John Patrick's
BLACKJACK

John Patrick's BLACKJACK

"So You Wanna Be a Gambler"

By JOHN PATRICK

A Lyle Stuart Book
Published by Carol Publishing Group

A Lyle Stuart Book
Published by Carol Publishing Group
Lyle Stuart is a registered trademark of Carol Communications, Inc.

Editorial Offices: 600 Madison Avenue, New York, N.Y. 10022
Sales & Distribution Offices: 120 Enterprise Avenue, Secaucus, N.J. 07094
In Canada: Musson Book Company, a division of General Publishing Company, Ltd.,
    Don Mills, Ontario M3B 2T6

Queries regarding rights and permissions should be addressed to Carol
Publishing Group, 600 Madison Avenue, New York, N.Y. 10022

Carol Publishing Group books are available at special discounts for bulk
purchases, for sales promotions, fund raising, or educational purposes.
Special editions can be created to specifications. For details contact:
Special Sales Department, Carol Publishing Group, 120 Enterprise Avenue,
Secaucus, N.J. 07094

Manufactured in the United States of America
10   9   8   7   6   5   4   3   2   1

ISBN 0-8184-0555-4

PREFACE

John Patrick's Blackjack is a book about betting on Blackjack. I don't know the exact number of people who play Blackjack in a casino, but I do know that the majority of them lose. Do you know why they lose? Because they do not understand either the theory behind the proper moves to make, or the way to manage money.

I will teach you how to win at Blackjack. The answers are all on these pages. You will learn the importance of the starting Bankroll, and also Knowledge of the Game to provide the theory behind every move you must make while sitting at a table.

But, most of all, you will learn Money Management and Discipline. These are the keys to any form of gambling that you undertake.

Since I concentrate on Blackjack in this book, you can rest assured that if you follow the rules which I have laid out, you will learn how to win.

Believe me, learning how to win is not an easy task. It takes practice, patience, and discipline. I will make you aware of how to acquire all of these.

If you are *tired of losing* and want to be a perfect Blackjack player, read *John Patrick's Blackjack*.

ACKNOWLEDGMENTS

A short, but sincere thanks to some people who contributed to the finished product of *John Patrick's Blackjack*.

My deep pride in being associated with the best group of instructors in the land: Joe Abrams, Les Scally, Mark Zimmer, Charley Zimmerman, Barry Urban, Greg Lentz, Ron Ludden, John Guibas, John Sullivan, Jim Gilrain, Jeff Dalia, Ron Olszowy, Austin Kosik, Carl Bajor, Jack Klarman, Bob Nash, Irv Hyatt, and the Las Vegas expert, Howie Goldstein.

And finally, there is no way this book could have been completed without the overall input of Jeff Mitchell, who kept me from drifting away from my main points of how to be a consistent winner.

These men have no peers as players or instructors.

CONTENTS

MONEY MANAGEMENT

DISCIPLINE

ODDS AND ENDS

INTRODUCTION TO GAMBLING

So You Wanna Be a Gambler

So, you wanna be a gambler? Well, you'd better be aware of what's in store for you. It's a tough business.

It's a challenge that can also be very rewarding. There are many people today who make a comfortable living gambling professionally. While most of them concentrate on a single game or sport, there are those who diversify on several different games.

There is one thing they all have in common: Whatever the game, they are experts. Now, I don't mean they're pretty good, or very good, I mean they're *perfect*! They know every facet of the game they play.

How about you? Do you classify yourself as an expert in any particular game of chance? If so, bet just on that game and nothing else; don't bet on everything you see.

For instance, if you are great at poker, make that your primary source of winning. If it is sports betting—say football—specialize in that. Of course, in order to be great, you must be an expert handicapper—not just an avid sports fan.

If you want to perfect casino games, then get ready for an exercise in practice, card recognition, and money control.

If you gamble, you have two choices: You can be an expert, or you can be a fool!

A professional gambler is an expert, or he doesn't stay in his profession very long. There are do's and don'ts in his business, and he knows every one of them. And, because he knows them, he avoids the don'ts. Rigidly. Automatically.

I hope you can avoid them, too. It will make you a winner. That's what this book is all about.

There are many things needed to become successful in gambling.

The main four (I refer to them throughout this book as the *BIG 4*) separate the professional from the amateur. They are:

1. Bankroll
2. Knowledge of the game
3. Money Management
4. Discipline

These are the sole ingredients of the winning formula for success in gambling. That's it! It will make you a winner. Abide by it and you're a pro. Ignore it and you're an amateur.

I don't know how many people will read this and scoff at the *BIG 4*, but I do know this: There are many who will not be willing to develop control. If you won't, you can't win. It's impossible to win consistently at gambling without an intelligent game plan.

Do you know what does you in most? Greed!

That's right, greed. It's first. Next is stupidity.

Every day I hear stupid statements. Some people who have been losing for years, come to me to find out if there is a way to win at Blackjack, or Craps, or Baccarat.

Do you know what some of these people tell me? "I guess I'm a bad player. You have proven to me that I had better improve my game, but it seems like too much work to learn everything about the game. Besides, I have trouble concentrating on too many rules."

And you know what? They can't bring themselves to practice discipline and learn how to win. But, they still go to the casinos, and they still get whacked!

If you want to gamble, decide for yourself how badly you want to win. The more you want to win, the more you have to follow the principles of the *BIG 4*. Not just casually, but to perfection.

All the answers are in this book. If the examples hit home, don't be upset. If you gamble, you probably make the same mistakes as your neighbors. The question is, how often do you make them?

Besides knowing the *BIG 4*, you must have a strong stomach. You're not going to win all the time, so when you lose, do it without grumbling. As the saying goes, if you can't stand the heat, stay out of the kitchen.

Ever go to the racetrack? If you do, you'll recognize the scenes I'm going to describe.

After every race, winners strut around like peacocks and proclaim their picks for the next race. And the suckers flock to these guys for advice.

Several years ago, I was at Monmouth Park with a friend of mine. His name is Bud-O. Well, Bud-O was in one of his usual slumps. Through the first five races, he didn't even have a horse show on the board. Before the sixth race he told me he was desperate to get a winner. You know what he did? He bet $10 to win on every horse in the race—a total of seven horses. I remember distinctly that the #1 horse broke out of the gate, went to the front, and stayed there for the entire race. It was the longest shot and paid $36 for every $2 bet on it to win. Bud-O collected $180 and was an instant hero with the horseplayers around us. Obviously, he didn't tell them he bet on every horse in the race.

Bud-O was now the resident genius. Everyone begged him for his picks in the seventh and eighth races. His choices all came in sixth or worse. He didn't wait to "help" with the ninth race. If he had, he probably would have been lynched.

People are so starved for winning, they will listen to anyone and base their bets on any advice (even bad advice). These people bet on someone's picks because they figure he is "hot."

Then, there are the losers. Excuses for not winning flow continuously. After a race, look around and see the sick expressions on people's faces. They complain that they were going to bet on a certain horse, but got a tip on another one. Or, they were shut out at the window. Or, the clerk gave them the wrong number. You name the excuse, and you'll hear it after every race.

The real problem is the lack of knowledge. People are too lazy to learn the game. And it's so easy! Betting is playing the percentages using simple, clear logic. It's plain common sense.

Want to be a gambler? Then zero in on the games you play best, and practice the rules of the BIG 4.

1. Bankroll
2. Knowledge of the game
3. Money Management
4. Discipline

If you're an expert at these, you'll be a winner. Consistently.

Don't dare go to a casino, or wager on a sporting event, or go to a track before reading this book. And if it doesn't jolt your senses with the first reading, read it again. This book can put an end to your losing. It stresses winning, discipline, knowledge—and most of all, money management! It covers all aspects of gambling, but concentrates on the primary problem confronting all people who gamble: How to win!!

I won't devote a lot of time to slot machines, or Roulette, or horseracing. The bottom line for all bettors is winning. So, I will emphasize the games which allow you a better chance of winning—or, to put it more accurately, the least chance of losing.

Blackjack, Craps, Baccarat, and Sports Betting are in this group. The percentage to the house (Vigorish) can be reduced low enough so that your staying power will be greater, and the opportunity to win will naturally increase. Remember this: The longer you can stay in a game—the longer you stay alive—the more likely you will be there when your streak comes.

I stress money management, and discipline, and learning how to win. If you can't learn how to win, if you can't acquire discipline, and if you can't manage your money—you'll be a hopeless loser. Learning how to win is an art. Once you master it, you'll never go back to being a loser.

When you finish this book, read it again, and again. Then go out and win!

INTRODUCTION TO GAMBLING

2

Expert or Fool?

We love it when our peers marvel at what an "expert" we appear to be in some endeavor, be it as a golfer, cook, hairstylist, artist, mechanic, mathematician, sailor—the list could go on and on.

We strive for perfection in whatever activity we undertake. We want to be perfect. The best. An expert.

Except when it comes to gambling! Suddenly, we assume we have all the answers. We no longer strive for perfection.

When you gamble in a casino, or on sports, or on anything, yours is an either-or performance. You are either an expert, or you are a fool.

That's true of many things we do, or try to do, during the course of our lives. The dictionary defines a fool as a person "with little or no judgment, common sense, . . ." The same dictionary says an expert is a person "very skillful, having much training and knowledge in some special field."

Take the case of an accomplished pianist—a person who has played and practiced for twenty years and now wishes to apply for a job with the Boston Symphony Orchestra. The day of the audition, he shows up and plays a number of compositions for the conductor. His only competition is a person who has played the piano for six months, having learned all he knows from a crash course he got through a money-back-guaranteed mail order ad.

Who is the fool?

As early as grade school and junior high, we begin training and studying and preparing for an occupation we hope to excel in. We read hundreds of books, spend long hours in the

5

library, seek out the opinions of "experts" in our field, and practice for years to sharpen our skills. This is true in medicine, law, teaching, music, sports—anything. We know that we have to be good to compete—to even get a chance.

Except in gambling!

All at once we're experts at gambling—sports, poker, horseracing, casino games. You name it.

I'd be guessing if I told you the exact number of people who bet or gamble each day. I don't know exactly how many. But if you think it's a minority, then your elevator doesn't go to the top floor!

The figure is in the millions. It can be lotteries, horses, numbers, casino games, or even bingo. We all love to gamble—to win a few bucks, to improve our finances.

Reasons vary, but I have found the main reason to be need! People need money. Gambling is exciting. It has a unique aura about it. It's entertaining. But people mostly gamble because they need money. Yet, they risk losing the very thing they are looking for: Money!

We are now back at square one. Only a fool would risk money on something he knows little about. Do you bet on things at which you are not an expert? Do you put out good money, hoping for a return on something in which your knowledge is even slightly suspect?

Stop and take a short quiz with fifteen questions. How many can you answer correctly?

Horseracing

1. What does "Grass Event" mean?
2. What does weight for age mean?
3. At what age can a horse run in the Kentucky Derby?
4. What is a gelding?
5. At what age can a horse run as a maiden?

Casino Games

1. Craps: What does "come-out" mean?
2. Craps: What percentage to the house (Vig) is there when

you place the 9?

3. Craps: How many ways can you make an easy 8?
4. Roulette: What is the payoff for a $5 bet on a column?
5. Blackjack: What is the best percentage move when you have two 7's versus the dealer's up card of a Queen?
6. Blackjack: What is the best percentage move when you have a 6 and a 3 versus the dealer's up card of a 3?
7. Baccarat: What is the payoff for a winning bet on the Tie?

Sports

1. What is the payoff, if you bet the underdog, in a proposition bet listed as Even-6?
2. If the Yankees play the Orioles in New York, and are listed as 7½–8½, what would you lay on a ten times wager if you bet the Yanks to win?
3. In football, what is the "rule of thumb" number of points allowed the home team when a betting line is made?

The answers to these questions are at the end of this chapter. If you got them all right, you are well above average in your knowledge of various forms of gambling. But answering these few questions does not necessarily mean you are an expert.

You need complete knowledge of every sport or game you play. If you don't know everything—I mean everything—about the game you bet your money on, you are a fool. You know the old saying: "A fool and his money are soon parted." Believe me, this is very true.

Stop for a moment and think of all the foolish bets you made in the past few months. A lottery in the office. A pool on a prize fight. The Super Bowl. Even a nickel and dime poker game.

Now think of your knowledge in the area you bet. Are you an expert in that field? Forget about the amount wagered. Even if it was only $5, you are throwing your money around on things that do not give you a good chance of winning.

If you are not an expert at Poker, don't play. Regardless of the stakes of the game—even penny ante—don't play unless you are an expert. Learn the game. Learn how to win and then play.

Good gamblers bet only on games where they have an advantage. They're looking for fools to play with. Don't make it easy for them.

Pick a game. Study it! Master it! Then play for money. But, only if you are equipped with the *BIG 4* (Bankroll, Knowledge of the Game, Money Management, Discipline).

You can become an expert in any game you choose. It beats being a fool.

ANSWERS TO QUIZ

Horseracing
1. Race run on grass, rather than on a dirt track
2. Weight a horse must carry based on its age
3. Three year olds
4. A castrated male horse
5. Any age, until it wins its first race

Casino Games
1. First roll of the dice to start a new game
2. 4%
3. Four ways: 2–6, 6–2, 3–5, 5–3
4. $10 (2–1)
5. Hit
6. Double down
7. 8–1

Sports
1. Even money
2. $85
3. 3

INTRODUCTION TO GAMBLING

3

Who Likes to Gamble?

It seems that every place you go, everyone you talk to is interested in gambling. How much money can I make? What do you have bet on the ball game? What do you have bet on the fight? Are you going to the racetrack? Are you going to Atlantic City? Are you going to Las Vegas? Almost every person is interested in some type of gamble, or way to make a couple of dollars. But only a few know how to win. That's right: *How to Win*!!

For years, I've watched people in Atlantic City, in Las Vegas, at racetracks. All trying to win money. I've said before that people gamble out of need. They need to win: To increase their financial status, to start a pot for retirement, to build up a next egg for the kids–or just to bring themselves up to the level of people they see, or read or hear about in the newspapers, on television, and on radio.

Most people who come to me are dying to win. They're really hurting. They've been losing for years. After a couple of discussions, they tell me I changed their entire approach to the game. They never knew what they were doing before. I frequently sit down in a casino and hear someone say: "I don't know how much I want to win, I'll play until I win everything I can."

Now that's someone asking for grief, and the casino will always be happy to oblige.

I'm not trying to discourage you from gambling. I'm trying to make you aware of things that cause you to lose. By eliminating bets that give you the least chance of winning, you increase your likelihood of making money by concentrating on the plays with the best percentage in your favor.

Personally, I think gambling—or the awareness of gambling—should be taught in high schools and colleges to make students wiser about one of life's major activities and something they'll undoubtedly be faced with. It's certainly as down-to-earth and relevent as "balancing a checkbook." In a short time these kids are out in the world. Warnings about how gambling "ruins lives" are not going to stop most of them from indulging in this so-called sin. Aren't they entitled to the best information available on the subject before getting involved? They deserve to be prepared.

In order to be a smarter player, you must begin with the four basic ingredients needed to be a successful player. Notice that I said player, not gambler. What I'm trying to do is teach you how to become a player. In a casino, the bosses consider a "player" a strong individual, someone who is tough to beat. They see the novice as a dummy, a jerk, a fool—someone who treats gambling as a lark, and blows good money.

The serious player? He (or she) is the one they fear and respect. They can tell a player by his money management, by the fact that he only wagers on games that provide him with an almost equal chance of winning—be it Blackjack, Craps, Poker, or Sports. He eliminates games that give him the least chance of winning, such a Roulette and Slot Machines. That's a player! When you are designated as a player by a professional gambler, you have "arrived" in the world of gambling.

Again, I list the four ingredients you must have:

1. Bankroll
2. Knowledge of the Game
3. Money Management
4. Discipline

If you have all four of these ingredients, you can win 60–70% of the time if you're willing to quit and accept a small percentage return of your starting bankroll. Having two or three of them isn't enough. Every wager you make should be backed up by the *BIG 4*.

I've said before the people bet out of need. I get the

opportunity to talk with different people each day. Students come from every walk of life: College students, senior citizens, professional men, housewives, etc. They are all looking for extra money. But most of them try for it the wrong way.

First, they start with a short bankroll. People try to make a killing with only two, three, or four hundred dollars. It's not going to happen—it can't happen!

The games of chance I suggest you play are Blackjack, Craps, Baccarat, and Sports. They are the ones that offer you the least chance of losing. But, if you don't have a bankroll, you can't compete; you can't stay in the game.

Recently, I was in a casino in Atlantic City, sitting at a $5 Blackjack table. At the table, was a young man, twenty-three or twenty-four years old, who had about $3,000 worth of chips in front of him. Next to him was a woman with about $300 worth of chips, plus two more who were betting $5 at a time. Everybody at the table had their eyes on the fellow who was betting $50 to $75 on each hand.

After thirty or forty minutes, I heard the woman ask the guy: "How much money do you want to win for the day?" He told her he wasn't sure; he planned to keep playing until his luck ran out. In other words, he was going to keep shooting and shooting for the moon, until either the casino closed its doors or he got wiped out. For the present, he was on some kind of roll. He won seven to eight hands out of every ten. I watched his style. He had the money, and he wasn't a bad player. But, not one of his bets was based on the count of the table, or his previous bet. He was betting strictly on hunches. He was able to stay in the game only because he had the bankroll. His knowledge of the game was OK; his money management was atrocious!

Listening to him tell the woman that he had no idea how much he was going to win or lose showed me he had no discipline. During the last several minutes I was at the table, his luck changed. He started losing. He increased his bet to $100 a hand, and then $200. He got surly as he continued to lose. He started making moves out of line with Blackjack percentages.

When I left the table, he had about $500 in front of him. He was yelling at the pit boss and wouldn't even talk to the woman sitting beside him.

This guy is so typical of the average gambler who loses control when the games goes sour.

Everybody likes to gamble. Everybody likes to win. But you're not going to win all the time. You can't. By perfecting your play at a certain game, having the proper bankroll, managing your bankroll, and disciplining yourself as to when you will quit, you will find how easy it is to win.

It is easy to gamble, but it is difficult to learn how to win.

Do you remember what the *BIG 4* is? Or, did you forget already? Memorize the *BIG 4*. You need them to play.

Not two of them, or even three—but all four. They are important. They will make you a winner.

INTRODUCTION TO GAMBLING

4

Vigorish (or Vig)

Have you ever heard the term Vigorish (or Vig)? You know what it means? It's the lousy edge against you. It's the juice which keeps the house operating.

If you go to a casino, or a racetrack, or even when calling your local bookie, it is this Vig that eats away at your bankroll. The bigger the Vig you give up, the quicker you will be eliminated from a game.

For example, at the racetrack (and depending upon the state you're in), an average of 18½% is taken from *every* bet pool (Win, Place, Show, Daily Doubles, Exactas, etc.) and never paid out to winning ticket holders. This is legally absconded with by the state and federal governments for taxes. Plus, the track also gets a share known as breakage. When the pie is divided, bettors share about an 81-cent slice for each dollar wagered.

That is some chunk to take off the top. The same is true whenever you play in a "house" game—the Vig pays for services you get: Lights, drinks, entertainment, etc. Anything that costs the house money.

Obviously, you want to play in games where the Vig is low.

Understanding all taxes and draws that come out of a game is not necessary. All you must know is which games provide the least built-in drain on your bankroll.

In a casino, you should know which of the many games have the lowest Vigs. These are the games to play. Avoid the others. Period! Avoid them!

The problem is that people don't avoid them. The games with the worst Vigs seem so simple, and you hear stories of

13

big scores being made, so you decide to try. Eventually, the Vig will eat up your bankroll.

Examine the casino games:

The Big Wheel   Good luck! You'll need it! The house has the best of it by almost 17%. This means that for every dollar bet, the casino returns 83 cents. Try dropping a dollar on the ground and picking up 83 cents. Over a period of time, won't your bankroll disappear? Of course it will.

Next time you are in Atlantic City, go to the Big Wheel, and count the number of spots. You will find fifty-four. The house pays 45-1 for the Jackpot Spot! Why don't they pay 53-1? That's the correct payoff. Well, the difference is Vigorish. Now count the $1 spots. A $1 bet pays even money for a winner. There should be twenty-seven ways to win that bet. How many ways are there?

Slot Machines   Notice the crowds at the slot machines. They're trying to overcome a Vig of about 13%. That's because the machines are set to return only 87% of the take. That's insane!

Anytime you gamble and aren't permitted to manage your money, you are forfeiting one of the keys to winning. In most casino games, you are allowed (although certainly not encouraged by the house) to increase your bet when conditions are in your favor, and vice versa. You can't do that with the Slots.

You say you don't know how to play the other games? Then don't play at all. You're bound to go broke if you challenge the Slots.

Roulette   The game of Roulette has a Vigorish of 5.26% on the Inside numbers and 7.31% on the five number grouping of 0–00–1–2–3. The Outside bets in Atlantic City have only a 2.63% Vig because they take only half your bet if 0 or 00 shows when you bet High, Low, Black, Red, Odd or Even.

I believe that this game gives you a shot, despite the 5.26 Vig on the Inside numbers, due to the multiple amount of plays that are available. The 2.63% Vig on the Outside bets is also not too shabby.

Since you have to be a perfect Basic Strategy player to get

the Vig in Blackjack down to 1.55%, then I'd push you toward Roulette because there are a lot of dorks at the Blackjack tables who think Basic Strategy is a five-year-old's first attempt to outwit his parents.

Roulette, you'll find out, is not as bad as the stories you hear about it.

Craps If you play only the Pass Line, and take free odds, the house advantage is a puny .8% (eight-tenths of one percent). It's not insignificant, because it still gradually erodes your bankroll. But, this is as good as it's going to get in a casino for you without a lot of study and special knowledge. It gives you a decent prospect for staying alive.

However, if you make bets all over the table—craps, hardway bets, placing the 4 and 10, etc.—the house Vig improves.

This is a good game to play. If you know how!!!

Blackjack This is *the* game to play if you are perfect. As I said earlier, not pretty good, but perfect. The card counter can get as much as a 2% edge on the casino.

If you do not know and practice Basic Strategy on every hand, you could be giving up a 30% to 40% advantage to the casino. This is the game where the house cleans up on the novice player.

The expert Blackjack player? The house fears him.

If you're not a card counter, but play Basic Strategy expertly and follow each and every move as taught in this book, you have reduced the Vig to only about 1½%.

If you are not a perfect Blackjack player, don't play at all. It is impossible to beat the house in the long run. It's hard enough for the expert. You can't have the edge if your knowledge of the game is limited?

Baccarat A good game. The percentage against you is only 1.38% if you bet *PLAYER* and 1.17% against you if you bet *BANK*. That is without knowing anything about the game. It is impossible to make a mistake. The rules of drawing cards are predetermined. But (and this is a big but) you must learn how to manage your money. Money Management is covered in later chapters.

Now you know what Vigorish is. Be prepared to deal with it. And stay away from games that have high Vigs.

BANKROLL

1

The Beginning

This is the start! It's the first pitch of a baseball game, the kickoff in football, the opening tip in basketball. It is part one of the *BIG 4*.

It may be only 25% of the total concept, but without it, you are unable to compete. Few people possess it. Even fewer can control it. It is the springboard to success! It is the bankroll!

What's a bankroll? If you think a bankroll has to be thousands of dollars, or some astronomical figure out of your reach, you're wrong. Dead wrong. A heavy bankroll can be as much as $5,000, and higher. A small bankroll is $300, but it is a bankroll just the same. A bankroll is the amount you take to the casino, regardless of how big it is.

As I said before, you need a bankroll to win. But, I didn't say you need an enormous sum of money to enter a casino. You can only play with what you have. If you have $300, that's your bankroll.

Naturally, the larger the amount of starting money, the more staying power you have, and the more relaxed you can play. I will go over ways to handle your bankroll, but for now, I want to correct mistaken ideas people have about money required for gambling. Obviously, you would love to walk into a casino with $5,000. You could play quite comfortably knowing you have such a nice cushion.

But the laws of economics and reality affect your life. You are restricted by what money you can use to gamble. This restriction destroys many people. They steal, lie, and cheat to get money to gamble. They lose, and try to get more capital. The down process has begun. For many, it's a one-way trip.

It is sad to hear numerous stories of broken lives, dreams, and families caused by this greed. The person will not stop gambling, and yet, if discipline and control could be developed, problems could be greatly reduced. The section on Discipline is very precise and should be carefully followed. I mention the discipline factor here because it ties in so closely to the bankroll.

I've heard hundreds of tales of huge bankrolls lost in casinos. In your own group of friends, there are probably several who have lost thousands of dollars gambling.

Sometimes these losses occur in the short span of two or three months, or maybe just a week. They get caught up in the game, lost a modest starting bankroll, say $600, and try to get it all back in a few hours. They invest more money in hopes of reversing their initial loss. Sometimes they get much of it back, run into a dry spell, and lose the second bankroll. Now they are down perhaps $1,500. They rehash their past sessions and remember the hot streaks. They reason that if they can just raise another $600 or $700 they'd have a chance to get another hot streak and recoup their losses. They pray for help and make promises that they will never again fall this far behind.

A new source is needed for the additional starting bankroll, even if it means selling something of value that belongs to the family, cashing in an insurance policy. Getting a personal loan. Taking out a second mortgage. Setting up a meet with the local loan shark at Vigorish that would horrify you.

The dastardly deed is done. Our hero has a fresh $1,000—a new start, big dreams, high hopes. He heads for the casino on cloud nine, grabs a seat at a Blackjack table and begins another session. With this new money, it'll be a cinch to rewin the lost $1,500.

Sure it will! In two hours he's broke. How can he explain $2,500 in losses to his family? How can he repay the loans? Panic takes over. His behavior is irrational. Every waking hour is spent trying to think of a way to win back that $2,500. It is a roller coaster ride to nowhere. If he is somehow able to get another bankroll and recover the $2,500, he will decide it is easy to win and will take another journey to dreamland, trying to break the bank.

You think this is an isolated case? I hear more confessions than a priest. People tell me very day of their experiences at the tables. This happens to be a true account of a man I know very well. He told me to relate these facts to wise up some other guy to the things that can happen when you lose control. On the day he started his particular slide, he suffered a $600 loss, after he had been ahead about $700. Was he content to walk away with a $700 profit? He was not! He wanted to own the left wing of that casino!

In two hours, he lost the $700 and then the original starting bankroll of $600. Not $590 or $575—but the whole $600. Every single penny of it. He bet right down to $5 on the last hand. Did he honestly believe he was going to win back everything, starting with a $5 win?

Right now, you may be dying to tell me about the time you won $700 starting with a $10 bankroll. Or, your neighbor won $4,000 at Craps by betting his last $2 on the Pass Line and letting it ride through twelve straight passes. Or, maybe you'll tell me about the old guy who put his last five quarters in the progressive slot machine and won a fortune! Wise up!! These are super rare incidents. Making a big comeback with a small bankroll can turn into wasted years and great sums of money being spent looking for a repeat. It would be cheaper if the comeback never came in the first place!

When I give open houses, or demonstrations, or lectures, I dread it when somebody announces he or she was at the casino last week and took out $10 and ran it up to $1,300. Or the guy who stubbornly proclaims, "I never lose at the casino." I ask him why is he listening to a lecture on gambling, and the reply is always the same: "I'm just curious to see what you have to say, but I don't need any help." Right away, the other people begin thinking that if it could happen to this guy, why couldn't it happen to them. They are then turned off to any thoughts of Discipline.

Do you know how long gambling has been going on? If the "house," or racetrack, or casino, or bookie joint wasn't winning so much money doing what they're doing, their owners and operators would find another line of business to get into.

They love stories being circulated about customers winning gigantic sums at the $5 tables. They make good publicity.

I am trying to change your attitude about gambling. I will teach you discipline. But, to get to the point of using Discipline, you must first have a bankroll. Again, you are back at the starting gate. What is a bankroll? You must supply the answer to that question. How much can you afford to put aside to gamble?

If you can afford to bring $1,000 to the casino, that is your bankroll. If you bring $800, that is your bankroll. If you can raise only $300, that is your bankroll. There is no way you can get around being short on money. You just have to accept it. How you manage it, will determine the extent of your success.

Assume Mr. A goes to the casino with $1,000 looking to win $500, and Mr. B goes with $300 and is also shooting for a $500 return. We have a discrepancy in goals.

At least one of them must be wrong. Either Mr. A is aiming too low, or Mr. B is aiming too high. Both can't be right. It's also possible they're both wrong! Mr. B, with the $300, is forgiven for having high hopes, but he's doomed if he enters the casino and pursues the same return as Mr. A, who has more than three times the bankroll. Mr. A is looking for a 50% return on his money, while Mr. B is shooting for more than a 100% return. Mr. B is in a dream world!

Bankroll is the key. The amount of your bankroll dictates how much you should expect to win. You will be given percentages later that translate into the exact dollar amount each of these men should plan to win. (Incidentally, both men *are* wrong. Mr. A, although seeking less than Mr. B., is still out of line looking for a 50% return.)

Remember the fellow I mentioned earlier? The one who fell $2,500 in debt by chasing his losses? I first met him when he came to a class of mine in Craps. At that time, he was over $13,000 in debt. These were gambling debts! His mind was in a complete state of flux. He was gambling every day, trying to win back some money. My first three meetings with him were devoted to discussing the theory of gambling. He knew

Blackjack basic strategy, Baccarat, and a little about Craps. He wasn't a perfect player, but he had a good grasp of the games. Later on, he would become an excellent player, but right now, the problem was making him recognize his shortcomings.

His biggest shortcoming? Bankroll!! He had absolutely no money to bet, but that didn't stop him from gambling. He kept going to Atlantic City with $40 and he kept getting beaten. That was before he and I became acquainted.

I helped him devise a plan of attack. He would concentrate on only three games whenever he went to the casinos. He would become an expert player at Craps, Blackjack, and Baccarat, and he would take exactly $100 when he went—no more, no less.

I insisted on two final conditions: (1) If he got ahead $25, he had to leave the casino. (2) If he lost $40, he also had to leave.

These conditions were binding. Either one would signal the end to his day.

As I write this book, it has been nineteen months since I first met him. He still goes to the casinos about three times a week. His starting bankroll is now $300—but his win goal is up to $60, and the amount he is allowed to lose is $120. His debts are down to about $7,000 and they keep dropping each week.

He drives a truck, visits Atlantic City often, and plays a mean game of gin rummy. He has learned how to win. He still has big dreams and big ideas, but he also has a small bankroll. He has learned to wait for his boat to come in. Someday it will.

Bankroll! You must have it to win. It's the beginning.

BANKROLL

2

Accepting Your Bankroll

Recognize and accept your shortcomings! If you don't have what it takes, get it or forget it!

The bulky 275-pound football player would like to be the glamorous tailback and score all his team's touchdowns, but he is forced to play tackle.

The five-foot, six-inch basketball player longs to play the pivot and wow the crowd with slam dunks, but he is made to play point guard and feed the rest of the team.

The plain Jane high school coed is dying to be homecoming queen, but instead is assigned to sell popcorn at the victory dance.

Like everyone else, these people have dreams, but are made to accept roles that are less than what they want. They accept the roles but swear to improve themselves. For the present, they make the best with what they have. Time and patient work can transform the future into something different. Tomorrow and each day thereafter may move them closer to the experience of a dream come true—or, may bring events to fashion a new dream.

The football player sheds a few pounds, works his legs into powerful pistons to become a college fullback, and he reads of his exploits on the sports page.

The basketball runt practices hard, develops some fancy moves to become the best in the land at his position, and hears the roar of the crowd.

The plain Jane enters womanhood, leaving behind her adolescent failings, and grows into an interesting and beautiful person who meets her Prince Charming.

Patience. They all had it to help them tolerate, but also over-come, their shortcomings.

Your bankroll is probably your shortcoming in gambling. How much must you have in your pocket when you enter a casino? What's the proper amount?

There is no proper amount. There is no hard and fast rule as to what you should start with. But you must accept what you start with as your own bankroll, and you must stay within its limits.

You think I'm going to tell Bertram Bigbucks that he can't take more than $900 to the casino? He'd laugh himself onto the floor of his twenty-eight-cylinder Rolls Royce.

Percy Pennywise can barely scrape up enough to take his three kids to a movie on Saturday. If I told him he couldn't go to Atlantic City with less than $900, he'd faint.

The decision is personal. Each player is different and will be limited by what he or she can bring to the casino. How you manage your money will determine your rate of success, but the importance of the starting bankroll can't be overem-phasized.

Going with too much gives a false sense of security and a tendency to "overspend" at the table. Going with too little causes a "scared" reaction, or panic, as soon as you lose a couple of dollars.

I resent jerks who write books about gambling and tell their readers to go to a casino with an amount of money they can "afford to lose." These poor people can scarcely afford to lose a dollar playing the lottery. And they are expected to believe nonsense about throwing away money they can "afford to lose"? No wonder the casinos win.

I've never yet heard a dentist say to a patient, "Well, you have a nice set of thirty-two teeth. You can afford to lose eight or nine of them."

Eighty percent of the people who come to me for help are $3 and $5 bettors. That is all their bankroll will allow them to play. Do you know how hard I have to work to convince these people to play at the table that is right for the size of their bankroll? Many feel that having a general idea about the game of Blackjack is sufficient to assure immediate winning results. They're wrong?

Winning is an art—like skiing. When you first learn to ski, don't you begin on the training slope? How about football players? Don't they scrimmage against weaker teams before they are sent into the Saturday fray? Even Muhammad Ali had his share of pushovers to see if he could win, before taking on the top contenders.

Where do you learn how to win? At the smallest tables. The casinos are going to be there for a long time. They'll wait for you. I would like to see you put aside a decent bankroll of maybe $800 or $900. Hopefully, it will take you long enough to save that much to keep you away from the tables until you master Basic Strategy—which you will find described in this book in great detail.

When you know Basic Strategy perfectly, and have $900, you'll be ready to attack.

First thing you do is break your $900 in half. Take $450 as your starting bankroll. Put the other $450 in a drawer somewhere to be used only when the starting bankroll is depleted. Here's wishing you'll never have to rely on the second $450.

If you can come up with a bigger stake, cut it in half. The amount is unimportant after you surpass the minimum.

Stuff your wallet with the $450 (or some larger starting bankroll if you prefer), plus a few bucks for chow and gas, and head for the casinos.

BANKROLL

3

Entering the Casino

You are outside the casino with $450 burning a hole in your wallet. It is decision time. Right here, preparing for battle, you must decide how much of a victory will satisfy you, or how much of a defeat will cause you to retreat.

Chapters on Money Management discuss amounts in detail. For now, accept the fact that you must have both minimum win and maximum loss figures to signal you when to quit playing. It is essential that you set these goals, and absolutely imperative that you don't forget them. Without win or loss figures in mind, you're inviting disaster. Right here in front of the casino, your decisions must be made, before you get caught up in the glitter and noise inside.

It is the lack of Discipline that destroys most players in gambling. Discipline is needed to quit when either a win or loss level has been reached.

As I have said before, I strongly urge that you be willing to settle for a conservative return on your investment. Since you have a bankroll of $450, your expectant win figure should be $90. That's a 20% return on your money.

I can hear the moans and groans. You probably want to double your money.

Well, face reality. Getting a 20% return on your money is quite an accomplishment.

I am not setting a win ceiling, only a win goal. The goal should be realistic, so it is within reach. Once you reach the goal, I will teach you how to pull back a certain amount, guarantee a win for the day, and then take your shot at bigger winnings. But first, back to basics:

Get to understand how difficult it is to win at casino games, but also appreciate that it is possible to win. Practicing the *BIG 4* makes it possible. If you think winning means at least doubling your money every time, you'll stay a loser.

The purpose of gambling is to take a certain amount of money into a casino and walk out with a profit. The more you bring into battle, the bigger the return. But, if you go with a small bankroll, then learn to live with a small return.

Inside the casino, your cash is converted into chips. The chips can deceive you about their worth. Nevertheless, you are playing with real money! Don't forget this fact for a single second, or those pretty colored plastic pieces will lull you into being reckless. *Monopoly money it ain't!!* It's the legal tender, the coin of the realm, the pay you earned with your sweat!

I've seen people with $1 chips get bored and start making crazy bets. They see other players with $25 chips, and get jealous. The atmosphere and sparkle of a casino influence and ruin many gamblers. That's why I insist you make decisions as to how much money you will lose, or win, in the sunlight—away from the glare and glamour.

You've been to the casinos before, haven't you? Do you ever set limits for yourself and then stick to them? I doubt it!

Discipline will turn your game around. Very few people set reasonable limits. Very few people win money in casinos—and wind up taking it home with them. There is a connection.

A $450 Bankroll is what approximately 70% of the people take to a casino. I have given you a 20% win figure. This is fair and realistic. Since there are so many people in this bankroll range, there are bound to be differences in opinion.

A small group of people will be content to win anything, and so a percentage win of 10% (or $45) would be plenty for them. There is nothing wrong with setting this low amount, and you should be able to hit it quite often.

You may turn up your nose at a 10% return on $450 because it sounds so small. Well, do a little arithmetic. Assume this $450 bankroll, with many 10% wins, will soon grow, within four or five months, into a healthy starting bankroll of $2,000. Continuing to look for a 10% return, you are now picking up a profit of $200 every time you win. All of a sudden, that size return looks good. Now the 10% is based on a $2,000 bankroll, and since the dollar return is higher, you overlook it being a low percentage profit.

Your total winnings increased because your bankroll increased. The percentage stayed the same, but now you are happy with the results.

To repeat: You have a small bankroll of $450. This is all you can put together. Yet, you are unwilling to accept a $45 profit. However, when that bankroll increases to $2,000 and the money return is greater—although it is still only 10%—you are satisfied. Carefully analyze the situation and you should admit that your attitude doesn't make sense.

If I gave you $100 and told you to go to a casino and win $10, you'd say it would be a snap. And it would be. But, you would be unhappy with a mere $10 profit. Would you be happy to win $200 a trip? You bet you would. Well, wait until you have a $2,000 bankroll, and go for the same 10% profit. You would then have $200.

Am I reaching you?

BANKROLL

4

A Proper Percentage Return

You must understand the importance of the bankroll. Everyone wants to win, despite comments of, "I just go for a good time," or, "I set aside an amount I can afford to lose."

Ridiculous! These people want to win, but don't know how. They honestly believe they are supposed to lose in a casino. That's because they never learned how to win. Think of all the times you went to a casino and were ahead $200 or $300. You believe it is your lucky day, and want to cash in big!

Victory dulls your thinking and you start increasing your bets, and turn into a different player. You reason that you are playing with the casino's money, so why not splurge? Well, throw out that theory! When you win, it's your money. It doesn't belong to the casino anymore.

What causes this sudden switch in tactics? This sudden increase in betting? Money! You now have more money sitting in front of you, and you lose all control.

Remember the emphasis I placed on the bankroll? I said the whole day started with the percentage of win placed on the amount of money you brought to battle. I suggested the decision of how much you wanted to win was based on your starting cache. That is why you make the decision early. It eliminates the chance you will make crazy bets when you are caught up in the excitement of the game.

Money does funny things to people. So does the lack of it.

I firmly believe people gamble out of need. Needs differ in amounts, but the ultimate purpose is the same. That is why so many of my lectures are devoted to making people aware of the proper first steps to winning.

Senior citizens I teach are very easy to convince. They want extra dollars to provide them with luxuries they normally can't afford. Their bankrolls are usually small. So they are easy to convince that to go for small percentage returns on a consistent basis is the proper approach.

Many of them begin with $200 as their bankroll. And it is a scared $200. They are terrified at the thought of losing. That is why they are receptive to control tactics.

You've seen players with $100 chips and stacks of $25 chips and it is very easy to be jealous. Some of these players bet amounts on a single hand that you would be content to win for the entire day.

But their method of betting is so slipshod and erratic that the bankroll they possess, though quite large, is not enough to make them win automatically. They don't know how to use their money wisely.

When I ask people how much they would be content to win on a given day, they say they don't have any idea. I get the same answer when I ask what their loss limits are. People tell me they never thought about it.

Well, if you are fortunate to have a big bankroll, you have the beginning of what could be a succession of winning days.

Treat that bankroll with great respect. As long as you have a bankroll, you will be able to compete, to stay in the game. Since I stress the importance of the bankroll, I also give you methods to protect it.

First of all, you don't want to lose the bulk of your bankroll at the first table, so you split it into three separate and equal sessions. A session consists of one-third of your starting bankroll. Always divide your starting capital into these separate sessions. If you take $600 to the casino, each session will begin with $200. If you bring $900, each session will be $300. If $300 is all you can afford, then $100 is the amount of each session.

Take an average figure of $600. That is the amount that best fits the $5 bettor, which most people are.

After splitting the $600 into three sessions, you make your way to the first table with $200. The remaining $400 is kept aside.

You don't have to guess what value table to sit at. The bankroll tells you.

To sit at any table, the preferred amount to have is forty times the minimum bet allowed. So, for a $5 table, this would be $200—which, multiplied by three sessions, translates into a $600 starting bankroll. The smallest amount you can take to a table is thirty times the minimum bet. That's $150 for a $5 table, and $450 for the starting bankroll.

Anything less than thirty times the table minimum is unacceptable for a session.

Ever see the guy who brings a $10 bill to the $5 table? Where is he going? He either gets enough to play sensibly, or doesn't play at all. This guy is trying to hold down his losses, but chances are he'll get wiped out. The small amount of playing money will soon cause him to play scared and affect his Basic Strategy moves.

If you visit the casino with a $300 bankroll, your sessions will consist of $100 each. Since that is only twenty times the amount of a $5 minimum bet, the $5 table is not for you. You must go to a $3 table. If there is none available, go to another casino. If you can't find an empty seat at one of the $3 tables, don't play. It's that simple.

These rules apply to all players. If you want to play at a $10 table, you should have $400 per session, and $1,200 overall.

TABLE MINIMUM	SUGGESTED SESSION	ACCEPTABLE SESSION	SUGGESTED BANKROLL	ACCEPTABLE BANKROLL
$3	$120 (40×)	$90 (30×)	$360	$270
$5	$200 (40×)	$150 (30×)	$600	$450
$10	$400 (40×)	$300 (30×)	$1,200	$900
$25	$1,000 (40×)	$750 (30×)	$3,000	$2,250
$100	$4,000 (40×)	$3,000 (30×)	$12,000	$9,000

If you don't have the minimum bankroll, wait until you do before going to a casino. Your sessions must consist of no less than thirty times the table minimum.

Many people ask me if it is acceptable to bring $200 to a

casino, and only play two sessions. It is impossible for them to scrape together the additional amount.

I tell them if they play only two sessions, they are depriving themselves of an extra session. Often, it takes until this third session to find a hot table. You are bending the rules because of a personal drawback. If you don't have all of the *BIG 4*—don't play.

BANKROLL

5

Scared Money

Without the bankroll, you can't compete as a gambler. Without the bankroll, you shouldn't try.

You've heard the term, "scared money." There is such a thing. It is surprising how many people play with scared money. They are petrified by the thought of losing. They make bets they consider "safe," instead of making good percentage moves.

Following are some bets that might be made by people betting scared. If you would make the same bets, look at your approach to the games you play.

1.   At the race track, you handicap the sixth race and come up with the probable winner. But the board shows him as a 14–1 longshot and you get scared. You lost the last four races and have only $10 left. You're scared to put it all on this longshot, because if it loses, you have to go home. You change your mind, throw out all your handicapping, and put the $10 on the 4–5 favorite. Now you feel safe because you have the horse that everyone likes.

You know the end of this story. The 4–5 horse runs a lousy race and comes in out of the money. The horse you originally picked jumps in front and wins by four lengths—and pays $31.40! You're sick, but you played scared. You don't even have faith in your own selections. Suffer!

2.   How about the weekly poker game? You've lost three straight weeks, and your confidence is shaken. It's the end of the month, you owe a car payment, and the rent is due. You really don't feel like playing as you're down to your final $100.

At the last minute you decide to go. Maybe you'll get lucky

and start a winning streak. Halfway through the night, you've managed to hold your own, and still have most of your starting bankroll. You're dealt three fours and feel quite happy. There's nothing out there that looks like a threat, but you decide not to bump the pot because you want to be able to survive the night. You just call every bet. The hand comes down to the last round, and you still have your three 4's. They guy next to you pulls a 5 for three of a kind. He beats you out and then tells you he was ready to drop at the first sign of a raise.

You played scared poker, didn't bet a bundle when you had the strong hand, and allowed someone to stay in and draw out on you. You played scared, and allowed your bankroll to determine your play. It cost you a pot. How many other pots did it cost you? Suffer!

3.   Maybe you're sitting at a Blackjack table. Your bus isn't scheduled to leave for an hour. You've had a rotten afternoon, losing everything except a paltry $40. You don't have the discipline to walk away when you're losing, so you decide to kill some time at a $5 table. First hand you get 11 against the dealer's 6. You're afraid to double down, as you want the $40 to last for an hour, so you call for hit. The dealer breaks and your winnings are $5 instead of $10.

Next hand you bet $5, get a pair of 3's against the dealer's 5, and again decide against splitting, and merely take a hit. Again, the dealer breaks, and you win another $5 instead of $10.

On the third hand, a $5 bet is made, and you are dealt a soft 14 (A, 3). The dealer has a 6 showing, but you figure he is due to win, and you don't want to risk that precious $5 chip. It will give you an extra hand to play. You again shun the double down and call for a hit. For the third straight time, you win and the dealer breaks.

You have won $15 in three successive hands that allowed either a double down or a split. If you were playing properly, you should have won at least three times that amount.

Again, it was the scared money that affected your thinking. Naturally, you have no Money Management, but it was your chicken-hearted approach that made you play like a fool. If it was early in the day, or if you had a bigger bankroll, you would have bet differently.

"Playing scared" is not only playing with a short bankroll, it's also playing with money needed for everyday expenses. Playing with scared money is a dangerous thing. It preys on your mind and weakens your game.

A big lesson in gambling: Don't play with a scared bankroll because you can't be competitive.

And if you can't be competitive, you're wasting your time and throwing away your money!

BANKROLL

6

Minimizing Losses

While we're still in the Bankroll section of this book, let's put something into your head right now: Gambling isn't a romp in the park with your best girl. It's not like having a candlelight dinner with Raquel Welch or having somebody throw a parade in your honor and hundred dollar bills at your feet.

In other words, gambling isn't all peaches and cream. Gambling is a war and if you're not prepared to take on those casinos with:

1. Decent Bankrolls
2. Perfect Knowledge
3. Strong Money Management
4. Strict Discipline

then you haven't got a prayer of winning. I'm talking about the *Big 4* and how important it is for you to have each of them.

It all begins with Bankroll and how you handle it. Holding your losses down keeps you in the game until a trend develops and your Money Management moves key you to decent returns.

But to stay alive at that table you have to be able to minimize your losses and that's where setting intelligent Loss Limits comes into play.

My friend Minny Mise is a tremendous blackjack player, but better than that she is a sharp manipulator of money.

When she loses three hands in a row she leaves that table quicker than a blink, without wondering what might happen if she stayed.

She holds her losses to a minimum and plays only where she is winning.

I want you to follow the lead of a gal like Minny Mise and concentrate on holding your losses down. It's a big, big, big key to winning. I wonder if you've got the guts to do it.

BANKROLL

7

Win Goals

These next two chapters are two of the most important in the whole book so don't just read them—devour the information. These are the two things that most of the dorks who gamble refuse to follow.

The first one is your Win Goal and it is the amount of money you set to win on a given day. But it should be an intelligent amount.

My friend Don DeGomb is a genius in the banking business but a gomb when it comes to gambling. He'll swing deals that save his bank hundreds of dollars by implementing some in-house controls.

But then he'll take a lousy $300 to a Blackjack table and try to win the east tower. Ask him what his Win Goal is and he'll give you that all-knowing wink and the soft elbow to the gut. Then this boob looks both ways to make sure no one is listening and whispers: "I just want to bring these guys to their knees by winning $10,000. That would make me happy."

Who does this clown think he's kidding? He isn't going to bring any casino to its knees with $300 or even $3,000. Maybe it'll drop to its knees begging him to come again with dreams like that but other than that it welcomes dorks who "go for the kill."

I want you to set a Win Goal based on your starting bankroll. The percentage won't sit well with you big dreamers like Don DeGomb but at least it is relatively close to a Logical approach.

A professional gambler sets 10% or lower as his Win Goal for a day and is ecstatic when he hits it.

He goes to a casino with $5,000 and hopes to win 6% or $300.

The novice goes to a casino with $300 and hopes to win $5,000. One of these characters is wrong.

I realize that most of you don't have the bread to bring a lot of money with you but I want you to realize that you only have a 50–50 chance of winning—if you're a perfect player—so how the heck can you expect to win zillions with pennies?

I've set 20% as your Win Goal and that's because I know you won't follow the true intelligent goal of 10%. You keep thinking gambling is your ticket to gigantic paydays and you're dead wrong . . . it isn't.

Gambling offers you a 50–50 chance of winning so if you can grab a 20% profit on a given day, you're a raving genius.

At this writing I've made twenty videotapes on gambling and written several books. All of them contain emphasis on Win Goals, Loss Limits, Money Management, and Discipline techniques. That's what gambling is. You aren't going to win billions but it will cut losses and allow you to pick up steady profits.

That's why I beg you to grab the message I'm trying to get across to you in all of these books and tapes: Set Win Goals and Loss Limits and quit with a profit on good days and quit on bad days before you go deep into the tank.

Your Win Goal should be 20% and when you reach that goal, rathole a percentage of that profit and play with the balance.

Win Goals. Set them and abide by them. Don't be a gomb like Don DeGomb, chasing the dream of fantasy.

Accept small consistent returns. When you do reach a hot streak, the dollars will pile up, but at least you'll have more days that kick off happy endings—if you'll only listen.

BANKROLL

8

Loss Limits

Probably of more importance is the setting of Loss Limits. These are stopgaps at a session where you have the guts to push yourself away from the table.

Les Branes is a fairly intelligent chap. He works hard, supports a family, coaches Little League, does work in his church and overall is a pretty sharp cookie.

But put Les Branes in a casino and he has less brains than his three-week-old canary. He'll buy in with $100, lose twenty hands in a row then slide off his chair looking to tell his tale of woe to anyone who'll listen: "Can you imagine, I lost twenty hands in a row—I didn't think it was possible." And then he laughs at his actions.

I think he's a dork. How could anyone lose more than four hands in a row without getting the message that the dealer is scorching hot.

Streaks dominate in gambling. When you're in a losing trend, you gotta run. Yet I see guys like Les Branes sit at a cold table and play down to their last chip.

Do they really think those last couple of dollars are going to turn that session around? Of course they do. And most people play to their last chip before they quit. That's their Loss Limit.

Well, I'm giving you a different one, and you'd darn well better grasp what I'm saying.

If you lost the first four hands of a session, you leave that table. Period. Four straight losses and you're gone.

Personally I use three. If I lose three straight, I'm history. Why sit there and be clobbered by a hot dealer? There are plenty of other tables.

You must also set a Win Goal of 20% and a Loss Limit. That limit is 40% in Blackjack. Craps, Baccarat, and Roulette have higher Loss limits of 50% and 60% but Blackjack is so tough that I give you 40% as your maximum loss before you pack it in.

You can make that Loss Limit 20% or 25% or 33% or anything lower than 40%, but not a dime higher.

That doesn't mean if you set the max of 40% and have lost 30% that you can say: "Well, if I lost 10% more I'll leave."

If you're getting whacked, get away from there. If some guy was popping you across the mouth, you wouldn't say: "Well, I'll just stay here until he draws blood."

Hey baby, that dealer who has banged you for a 30% bite is drawing blood. You just haven't got the brains to know it.

The failure to set Loss Limits is a drawback of 90% of people who gamble. They just don't realize that somewhere else in that casino is a cold dealer, just waiting to be beaten.

One more point. If you bring $100 to the table and lose 40%, then the $60 balance should be put in your pocket, never to be touched again that day. Period.

And don't bring $40 to a table and tell yourself you really have $100 and this would have been your Loss Limit anyhow. It is easier to accept losing 40% of $100 and putting $60 in your pocket then losing your whole $40 and leaving the table broke.

It is a psychological approach but it's true. The feeling of getting wiped clean is devastating.

Finally, for you sharp people who understand the importance of Loss Limits, set lower amounts like 25% or 30%. It'll be easier to climb back at another table then if you're a bundle in the hole. A lot of people lose so much at the first session, they can't recover.

Loss Limits—another big key to successful gambling. Will you listen and set these limits? Will you? I doubt it—and that's why you lose so much so often.

BANKROLL

9

Wrapping up Bankroll

This won't be a long message and it shouldn't be. It is so important that you realize how vital it is that you have a decent amount of money to battle with.

Most people go to a casino with four $10 bills, a handful of singles, three roles of nickels, two Indian-head dimes, and a used stamp. Where are you going with that mess?

To top it off, that guy is looking to make his car and mortgage payments with his profits. He's dreaming.

Most people don't have the proper bankroll. I can accept that and also sympathize with those people because I went through those same periods myself. And it led me to play like a dork.

So if you don't have the proper bankroll, do one of the following:

1. Don't play until you have the right amount,
2. Accept a return, based on the amount you do have, regardless of how small it may be.

I hope you'll listen to this advice, because bankroll is the start of your day. Look back over these chapters, especially the ones on Win Goals and Loss Limits.

When you grasp this message, you can move on to Knowledge of the Game.

KNOWLEDGE
OF THE GAME

1

Blackjack

Do you know what Blackjack is? Do you know what you're doing when you sit at a Blackjack table? I hope you do.

A lot of people go to a casino and think they know the game. Yet, some of them don't realize that when the dealer has Blackjack and they have 21 with three or four cards, that the dealer wins the hand. They think it's a tie.

I hear people ask dealers, "Do I win with five-card Charlie?" "Do you still have surrender?" "Do you hit 17?" "Can I split this hand?"

I can't believe these people are willing to put their money in front of them without knowing the rules of the game?

This book does not attempt to teach you everything there is to know about the game of Blackjack. There are card counting strategies and other subtleties of the game which are best taught in a school.

What this book does attempt to do is fine-tune your game in certain areas and emphasize a conservative style of playing.

I also promise to make you an expert in *Money Management* and *Discipline* if you are willing to faithfully obey the rules in those sections.

What is Blackjack? Blackjack is an Ace, and either a 10, Jack, Queen, or King. The object of the game is to get as close to 21 as possible without going over. If you wind up with a hand that's higher than the dealer's, and you didn't exceed 21, you win and get an even money payoff for your bet, and in most casinos you'll get 3–2 for getting a Blackjack (as long as the dealer doesn't have one).

All of the cards in the deck are equal to their face value,

except for the Ace. The Ace can count for 1 or 11, at the discretion of the player. As for the dealer, if he has a "soft" 17, he must stand. This is because the rules in Atlantic City and Las Vegas state that the dealer must stand on all counts of 17, hard or soft.

A hard 17 is a 10 and a 7—a soft 17 is an Ace and a 6. When you have an Ace in your hand, it is called a soft hand because you have the option of using the Ace in a soft or flexible manner, either as a 1 or 11. For example, if you had 2–A–2–3–A, your hand would total 9 (if you count both Aces as one) or 19 (if you count the first Ace as one and the second as 11).

In the next chapter is a Basic Strategy chart based on percentages obtained by playing billions of simulated hands on a computer. The program was developed by Julian Braun, an expert from IBM. I have slightly modified Braun's recommended moves for the chart to reflect my own theory of conservative play.

KNOWLEDGE
OF THE GAME

2

What Is Basic Strategy?

Basic Strategy consists of the best percentage moves of drawing a card, standing, splitting, or doubling down, after you receive two cards and the dealer reveals his up card.

Early in the 1960s, an IBM computer expert named Julian Braun ran some 9,000,000,000 (that's nine billion!) combinations of a player's hand against every possible up card for the dealer, based on one-, four-, six-, and eight-deck games.

His findings are usually the basis for most of the moves a good player will employ in a casino.

I teach most of Mr. Braun's basic Strategy moves, except in the cases where I favor a more conservative brand of Blackjack (when the dealer is in a strong position). I also preach a more aggressive style when the dealer is weak.

The chart in this chapter shows your moves against a neutral deck. A neutral deck is the condition you are faced with during the first several hands after the dealer shuffles, regardless of how many decks are used. These moves will vary for card counters, who modify the ways they play according to the richness or poorness of a shoe. When you memorize this chart, it will be a giant step towards cutting your casino losses.

Glance at the chart and notice its patterns. Most splits and double down moves occur when the dealer's up card is 2, 3, 4, 5, and 6. This is because he's in trouble when he shows one of these cards—so go straight for his jugular.

When the dealer shows 2 through 6, he is said to be in a breaking position. That means he is likely to turn over a card that will make him exceed 21. The only way the dealer can be busted and automatically lose is if he takes a hit (no two cards can add up to more than 21). According to the rules, the dealer

43

must hit if he has less than 17.

Whenever a 2 through 6 is showing, you know he must take another card because no combination of two cards, where one of them is 6 or less, can add up to 17. The lone exception to this is the soft 17. So, when the dealer shows a 2 through 6, the trick is to stay in the game as long as you can against his weakened position.

Remember, there are thirteen cards a dealer can turn over as his up card. Ace through King. Of these, only five make him obviously vulnerable (2, 3, 4, 5, and 6). The 7 and 8 are considered neutral (neither strong nor weak). Respect the 7 and 8, but don't fear them.

The up cards to fear are 9, 10, J, Q, K, and A. When he turns one of those cards over, he might as well put a gun to your head. You're in trouble!

By simple arithmetic, you can see that you're in trouble six times, as compared to his being bad off only five times. And you're not exactly swinging on a star when he shows a 7 or 8. The edge is clearly his after each side has been dealt two cards. The reason you're at an additional disadvantage is because you must decide on hitting or not hitting potential breaking hands before he does. You are susceptible to busting before the dealer turns over his down card.

So what do you do about it? You learn Basic Strategy. You learn how and when to double down and split when he is in trouble. Without these strong moves, and the opportunity to double your bet when he is in trouble, it should be obvious he will put you away if you continue to play him head to head.

You must learn to take advantage of him when he is weak. The good, strong Blackjack player knows this. The novice doesn't. Guess who gets destroyed?

Divide this chart into four sections. Concentrate on one section each day and then tie them together. Devote three fifteen-minute periods a day until you master it.

The sections should be:

  8 through 11
12 through 17
A2 through A7
A8 through 10-10

Perfect this Basic Strategy!!!

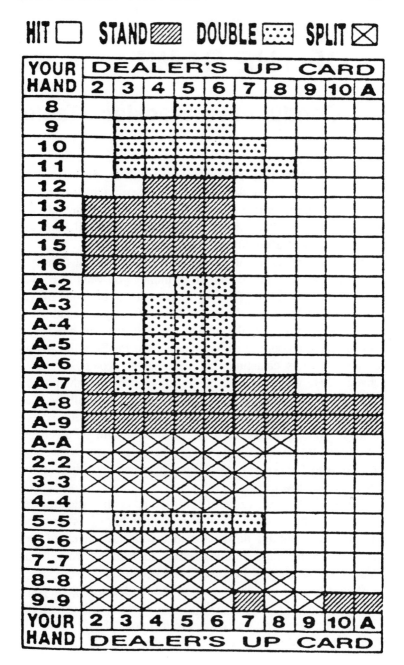

HIT ☐ STAND ▨ DOUBLE ⊡ SPLIT ⊠

YOUR HAND	DEALER'S UP CARD									
	2	3	4	5	6	7	8	9	10	A
8				DOUBLE	DOUBLE					
9		DOUBLE	DOUBLE	DOUBLE	DOUBLE					
10		DOUBLE	DOUBLE	DOUBLE	DOUBLE	DOUBLE				
11		DOUBLE	DOUBLE	DOUBLE	DOUBLE	DOUBLE	DOUBLE			
12			STAND	STAND	STAND					
13	STAND	STAND	STAND	STAND	STAND					
14	STAND	STAND	STAND	STAND	STAND					
15	STAND	STAND	STAND	STAND	STAND					
16	STAND	STAND	STAND	STAND	STAND					
A-2				DOUBLE	DOUBLE					
A-3			DOUBLE	DOUBLE	DOUBLE					
A-4			DOUBLE	DOUBLE	DOUBLE					
A-5			DOUBLE	DOUBLE	DOUBLE					
A-6		DOUBLE	DOUBLE	DOUBLE	DOUBLE					
A-7	STAND	DOUBLE	DOUBLE	DOUBLE	DOUBLE	STAND	STAND			
A-8	STAND	STAND	STAND	STAND	STAND	STAND	STAND	STAND	STAND	STAND
A-9	STAND	STAND	STAND	STAND	STAND	STAND	STAND	STAND	STAND	STAND
A-A	SPLIT	SPLIT	SPLIT	SPLIT	SPLIT	SPLIT				
2-2	SPLIT	SPLIT	SPLIT	SPLIT	SPLIT	SPLIT				
3-3	SPLIT	SPLIT	SPLIT	SPLIT	SPLIT	SPLIT				
4-4				SPLIT	SPLIT					
5-5			DOUBLE	DOUBLE	DOUBLE	DOUBLE	DOUBLE			
6-6	SPLIT	SPLIT	SPLIT	SPLIT	SPLIT					
7-7	SPLIT	SPLIT	SPLIT	SPLIT	SPLIT	SPLIT				
8-8	SPLIT	SPLIT	SPLIT	SPLIT	SPLIT	SPLIT	SPLIT	SPLIT	SPLIT	SPLIT
9-9	SPLIT	SPLIT	SPLIT	SPLIT	SPLIT	STAND	SPLIT	SPLIT	STAND	STAND
YOUR HAND	2	3	4	5	6	7	8	9	10	A
	DEALER'S UP CARD									

KNOWLEDGE OF THE GAME

Conduct at a Blackjack Table

Do you know how to conduct yourself in the casino? Pit bosses, boxmen, and dealers will give you the respect and courtesy you're entitled to. Act like a gentleman or lady and you'll be treated like one. Act like an ill-mannered boob and you'll be treated accordingly.

When you sit down at a Blackjack table, the first thing you should do is take out the amount of money you want to convert into chips, say $100. Put the money down in front of you because a dealer is not allowed to take it from your hand.

The dealer will take the money, lay it in front of him, count out the same amount in chips, then tell the Pit Boss the amount of money he is changing. In this case, he would say "$100 change." He will wait until he gets clearance from the pit boss and then put your $100 in chips in front of you. Pull the stack close to you and place your bet on the layout in the spot in front of you. When the cards are dealt, you will be given two cards face up (Atlantic City rules—the rules vary from casino to casino in Las Vegas). The dealer gets one card face up and another face down.

Don't touch your cards! (Again, this is an Atlantic City rule.) All signals to the dealer regarding hitting, staying, or splitting and doubling down, are done with movements of your hand or by placing additional chips in front of your cards. Also, don't touch your bet once it has been made!

If you touch your cards or bet, the dealer will give you a polite warning. Perhaps he'll give you two polite warnings. Beyond that, you're exceeding your quota. Don't force the dealer to scold you a third time; you'll make him angry.

Nobody likes an angry dealer.

If you are a smoker, show consideration for the people next to you by asking their permission to smoke. If they object, don't smoke or go where you can. Some casinos now have smoking and no smoking tables, so take note of which one you're at.

Don't carry on unnecessary conversations. It's distracting to other players. Besides, it's extremely difficult to chatter and concentrate on your cards at the same time. What do you want to be? A socializer or a smart player?

Don't be a cry baby.

Don't ask for the waitress every two or three minutes.

In general, don't be a nuisance. Acquire the conduct and class that will make you welcome in the casinos.

KNOWLEDGE OF THE GAME

Some Terms and Some Rules

Here are some Blackjack terms and rules:

Cut Card A plastic card that the dealer inserts into the decks after the cards are shuffled. In a six-deck shoe, the cut card cuts off about two decks. This is done to thwart card counters.

Double Down To double your original bet after you have been dealt your first two cards. Suppose you are given a 6 and 3 as your first two cards. If the dealer's up card is a 3, 4, 5, or 6, you will want to double your bet because he is in trouble with a "poor" or "weak" card showing. In Atlantic city, you can double down with any two cards dealt to you. If you wish to double down, place an amount equal to your original bet next to it. If you bet $10, you can bet another $10 on a double down. When you double down, you will be dealt one additional card to complete your hand.

Doubling for Less Suppose you bet $10 and the dealer gives you a 6 and a 5 (11). The dealer's up card is an 8. You know you should double down, but you're afraid he may beat you. You want to double down for less to be safe. Say, $5 instead of $10. Is this allowed? Yes! Is it a smart move? No! If you have the dealer in trouble, go for his throat. Either the play calls for a full double down, or no double down. There is no such thing as an educated half-hearted double down. When you double for less than the full amount, you show your ignorance.

Face Up Deal In Atlantic City and most of the larger Las Vegas casinos, both of the player's cards are dealt face up. The dealer has one card dealt face up, and the other card dealt face down.

Hole Card   The dealer's hidden card.

Insurance   To "insure" a hand against the dealer drawing a Blackjack. Read the chapter on Insurance to learn all you need to know about this subject.

Push   A tie hand. Neither you nor the dealer wins.

The Seventeen Rule   In American casinos, the rules state the dealer must stand on all 17's. Even if a player's open hand shows 18 or higher, the dealer must stop on 17.

Shoe   A plastic box where the dealer keeps the decks of cards during the play of the game.

Signals   In Atlantic City, don't ask the dealer for a hit or tell him you want to stand. All actions should be signaled to the dealer with your hand. Tap the table next to your cards to indicate you want to draw a card; wave your open palm over your cards to signify you don't want anymore cards.

Splitting   All casinos allow you to split pairs when they are the first two cards. The chapter on splitting details when to make this move.

Stiff Hand   A bad hand, 12 through 16.

KNOWLEDGE OF THE GAME

5

The Dealer's Up Card

No matter how many decks are used in a Blackjack game, when the cards come out of the shoe there are only 13 possible cards that can be dealt: Ace through King.

Whether the card is up or down, it can be only one of 13 kinds—the suits are meaningless.

This is true of the dealer's up card as well as any other card. Every decision you make in Blackjack is based on your hand versus the dealer's up card. So, it's absolutely required that you become able to recognize each card and its potential threat to you.

If the dealer shows:

Ace—You're in the worst trouble there is!

10-King—Conditions aren't much better.

9—The dealer is still very strong.

8—Respect him, but don't fear him.

7—A little respect, but he is getting weak.

6—Now he's in trouble. Go for the kill!

5—He's still in big trouble. Play aggressively.

4—He's still weak.

3—He can break, but be less aggressive.

2—He's still weak, but show some respect.

This is a capsule of the dealer's strength based entirely on his up card. You can't see his buried card, so forget about trying to guess what it is.

(9 through Ace) Separate in your mind his strong cards from the others. When he has a 9 through Ace showing, you are going to lose a majority of the hands. On an average, he will

turn one of these six strong cards over six out of thirteen hands. Be prepared for it. It's going to happen and there is nothing you can do to prevent it.

(7 through 8) The 7 and 8 are called neutral cards. The dealer is neither weak no strong. But, show respect for these cards, especially when you are in a breaking situation.

(2 and 3) The 2 and 3 are also considered chancy situations and tough to gauge. Many players get overly aggressive against these cards, and end up getting hurt. Agreed these are breaking hands and the dealer is in trouble, but I am warning you to double down only when my Basic Strategy chart tells you to.

(4, 5, and 6) This is what you are looking for. This is when you must attack the dealer. Remember, he will have these up cards only three out of thirteen hands, so you must take full advantage of the few times they will appear. Unfortunately, he'll get the 9-A twice as often.

The thirteen possible up cards can be divided into these four groups:

9-A—You are in trouble.

7-8—Neutral.

2-3—Dealer is weak, but respect him.

4-6—Dealer is in trouble.

The average winning hand is 18½. If you have 17, you have nothing. And 18 can be best described as "next to nothing."

Since 17 and 18 are nothing hands, what do I recommend you do when you get them? Nothing! There is nothing you can do with those hands. Surely you can't hit them.

The next time you are in a casino, watch how many times 18 fails to hold up. It is just not a strong hand.

Even more frustrating is a 17 hand. You'll lose more often with it than you will with an 18 and you still can't hit it.

The dealer will get a powerful up card an average of six out of thirteen hands, and he'll win most of them. What can you do to compensate? Get him when he is weak by splitting and doubling down and using skillful Money Management.

Since the 7 and 8 are considered neutral, you must wait patiently for the 2 through 6 (mostly 4-6) to show up. This is when he is vulnerable. This is when you must strike.

Many people, when they get an 11 against the dealer's 9 or picture card or Ace, immediately shove out that extra bet to double down. I strongly advise against it. Double down only when the dealer is weak.

Once you have memorized my Basic Strategy chart, don't deviate from it. Expert card counters are permitted to make minor strategy changes. Unless you are willing to invest the many hours of study and practice it takes to become a superb card counter, don't make any changes!

KNOWLEDGE OF THE GAME

6

Surrender

Don't skip this chapter. It is a very controversial subject, yet something that I am strongly in favor of.

It is a rule that was put into play when the casinos first opened in Atlantic City and then disappeared for awhile amid a lot of behind the scenes mumbo jumbo.

The rule is called Surrender and it allows the player the right to give up half his bet in situations where he feels he has a difficult chance of winning.

For instance, you are dealt a hard 16 and the dealer shows a power card of Queen. You've bet $5 on that hand. You can play it out and be in a position where you will lose 75% of the time if you hit and 77% of the time if you stand.

In layman's terms, you have eight 250-pound gorillas coming at you and you're standing on a cliff. You're dead if you stand and fight; you're dead if you run.

If they allowed you to surrender, you'd give up half your money and maybe get a black eye. It beats getting clobbered.

I suggest Surrender. With that hard 16, the dealer would take $2.50 and give me the other half. However, if he turns over his buried card, and he has Blackjack, all decisions are off and you lose the whole $5.

Many "experts" hate surrender because they claim you have to lose 75% of those situations to make it viable. But their statistics are based on thousands and thousands of decisions.

My contention is that if Jackie Black is playing BlackJack and is dealt a hand of 15 against the dealer's power card, he's in trouble and forget the computer crap. What'll bail him out of that particular hand? Surrender minimizes the loss and I *strongly* am in favor of holding down losses.

At this writing, not all casinos in Atlantic City have Surrender. Several new ones are contemplating putting it in to stimulate business, because 90% of the people don't even understand how to use it, so you'll find a couple of casinos in Atlantic City with it.

In Vegas and points West, only a handful of the casinos use it and it's up to you to find out which ones.

As I stated before, I am a billion percent in favor of you using it. In fact, I wouldn't dream of playing a hand of Blackjack unless they allowed Surrender.

That's why I give credit to any casino that offers the option.

The following are the hands I suggest you Surrender:

Surrender	vs. Dealer
Hard 4	9 through Ace
Hard 5	9 through Ace
Hard 6	9 through Ace
Hard 7	9 through Ace
Hard 8	9 through Ace
Hard 14	9 through Ace
Hard 15	9 through Ace
Hard 16	9 through Ace
Hard 17	9 through Ace

Yes, I said 17. Work it out for a couple of hundred hands. Give yourself 17 and the dealer a 10. Turn over fifty hands. See what happens. Play out each of those hands against the dealer's up card of 10. You'll surrender 17!!!

Surrender. It's a powerful tool for the Blackjack player. Use it!!!

KNOWLEDGE OF THE GAME

7

Doubling Down

A strong Blackjack player must know when to double down. It is a very important move!!!

Check my chart and you'll see most doubling down plays are when the dealer has a 5 or 6 as his up card. Next, we attack the 4, then the 3, and finally the 2 and 7. Against the 8, there is only a token attack.

Most people think doubling down is done when you have a better chance of beating the dealer. This is technically inaccurate. What you really look for are opportunities to increase your bet when the dealer is most likely to go bust.

You are in trouble when the dealer shows 9 through Ace. Therefore, when he's weak, you must bet more money against him. Otherwise, you have no chance of leaving the table a winner.

Imagine you are dealt a 5 and an Ace for a soft 16. The dealer's up card is a 5. You know he is in trouble.

You feel pretty cocky because my chart tells you to slide out another bet and double down. What will you get as your final hand? (Remember, the average winning hand is 18½.)

The dealer hits your Ace, 5 with:

    5—You have 21 (very strong)
    4—You have 20 (strong)
    3—You have 19 (still pretty strong)
    2—You have 18 (less than the average winner)
    Ace—You have 17 (a nothing hand)

All other card possibilities (6–K) will give you a trouble hand.

This is a typical example of doubling down, where you wind up with a bad hand eight out of thirteen times and a neutral 17 and 18 once each. If you can expect only three good hands out of thirteen, why is doubling down such a strong move in this situation?

Well, the dealer faces the probability of similar rotten combinations. And, any time he hits again (because he's still below 17) further increases his chances of busting.

The idea is to keep your bets down until the dealer is in trouble, and then sock it to him! He should be in trouble several times each shoe. When he is, and you have the proper cards to allow a double down against him, don't be a coward. Go after him!

KNOWLEDGE OF THE GAME

8

When You Have Eight

When you have a hand totaling eight and the dealer's up card is anything but a 5 or 6, I say hit. When he has a 5 or 6, double down.

This is contrary to what other Blackjack experts recommend, but I believe you should have as much money bet as possible when the dealer shows the weakest cards. This is the only reason you double down. From a percentage standpoint, over hundreds of hands there is a slight advantage in hitting rather than doubling; however, during a short session, this small difference is outweighed by the likelihood that these situations will arise very few times—if at all—and I prefer to attack the dealer with the biggest weapons in my arsenal whenever he is vulnerable.

If you ever have an opportunity to discuss the strategy of doubling down and splitting with card counters, you will discover that many of them not only double down with eight and nine, but also seven, when the dealer shows a 5 or 6—and when the shoe is "rich" (full of ten-count cards) compared with a neutral condition.

The theory is simply that you must get as much money bet against the dealer when he is in trouble.

This probably doesn't make sense to you since you already know that 18½ is the average winning hand, and you should be striving for at least 19. Why would any sane person double down with 7 when no single card in the deck can transform 7 into 19?

To repeat myself, you do not double down to improve your hand. You double down to increase the amount of money wagered against the dealer when he is in trouble.

That's why when the dealer shows a 5 or 6, and you have 8, you should always double down. The 8 can be any of the following two-card combinations: 2 and 6, 3 and 5, 4 and 4. (Splitting fours against the dealer's 5 or 6 is not a bad move, but you should only do it when you become a card counter.)

BASIC STRATEGY WHEN YOU HAVE EIGHT

DEALER'S UP CARD	YOU SHOULD
5 or 6	DOUBLE DOWN
2–4, 7–Ace	HIT

KNOWLEDGE OF THE GAME

9

When You Have Nine

Not a shabby hand.

If you double down with nine and draw a 10 or a face card, you end up with 19. Pretty good. Get an Ace and you have 20. That's better.

Double down with 9 when the dealer shows 3 through 6. When he shows 7 through Ace, or the troublesome deuce, don't double down—take a hit!

Resist the temptation to double down when the dealer shows a 7. Any card from a 2 to a 7 would lock you into a hand of 16 or less. The dealer would beat you with a standing hand of 17 or 18 if his hole card were a 10, or picture card, or Ace. The percentages prove it's not worth the risk to increase your bet.

Hit nine against the 2 and 7, and of course, the 8 through Ace. Double down against 3 through 6.

BASIC STRATEGY WHEN YOU HAVE NINE	
DEALER'S UP CARD	**YOU SHOULD**
3–6	DOUBLE DOWN
2, 7–Ace	HIT

KNOWLEDGE OF THE GAME

10

When You Have Ten

I am a cautious Blackjack player. My conservative moves frequently produce a raised eyebrow or two. One of the critical situations where this is almost a certainty is when you hold a two-card total of 10.

In this situation, my Basic Strategy chart tells you to double down against the dealer's up card of a 3 through 7 and hit against the 8 through Ace.

Julian Braun has shown that the percentages slightly favor doubling down with a 10 versus the 8 and 9, but my objective is to limit your losses with less aggressive moves.

Also, with a poor deck, I won't double a 10 against a 2. But you can't know a deck is poor unless you know how to count cards. So, for now, stick with doubling down a 10 against a 3 through 7, otherwise, you must hit.

BASIC STRATEGY WHEN YOU HAVE TEN

DEALER'S UP CARD	YOU SHOULD
3–7	DOUBLE DOWN
2, 8–Ace	HIT

KNOWLEDGE OF THE GAME

11

When You Have Eleven

This is much like 10, except you should double an 11 against 3 through 8 and hit against the 9 through Ace. And again I can hear the experienced Blackjack player let out a yell! Not versus the Deuce?

I don't like to attack the dealer when he has a 9 through Ace showing. If that's the way I play, why would I tell you to play differently. I imagine your money is just as important to you as mine is to me.

Whenever I sit in a casino and see players doubling down with 10s and 11s against the dealer's 10 or Ace, I look away. It's too difficult to compete against a power up card by trying to improve a 10 or 11 with only a one-card hit. And that's all you get when you double down–one card!

Some time ago, I appeared on a radio talk show in New York and one of the questions was from a woman who wanted to know what she should do with an 11 against the dealer's 9. I told her to hit and she told me that all the books she had read advocated doubling down. I asked her if she was winning in those situations and she said she was losing most of the time, but was afraid to vary from advice she had been following for so many years: "Always double down with eleven." Well, I gave her new advice. And that advice also goes for you if you think the same way she did.

I don't know if I convinced her, but while I was talking to her, a man from Middletown, New Jersey, was also listening to the broadcast.

The next day he came to sign up for a class I was teaching. He said he had read six or seven books on Blackjack and they all urged doubling down with 11—always! This man was fed up with that particular strategy because it was beating him. He wanted me to teach him my way because I was the first "expert" he ever heard of who dared to have a different idea.

People have been told over and over that they should always double down with 10 and 11. I stress a more conservative style of playing.

For you novices who are being introduced to the game, follow my Basic Strategy. When your first two cards add up to 11, double down only when the dealer shows 3 through 8—hit against 9 through Ace.

How about you experienced players? Try it my way for two months. Record your wins and losses when the "eleven" situation arises. You'll be pleasantly surprised at the results.

BASIC STRATEGY WHEN YOU HAVE ELEVEN

DEALER'S UP CARD	YOU SHOULD
3–8	DOUBLE DOWN
2, 9–Ace	HIT

KNOWLEDGE OF THE GAME

12

Breaking Hands:
Twelve–Sixteen

You've heard the term "breaking hands" many times. Be sure you know what it means:

1. When you are dealt a 12 through 16 count for your first two cards, you have what is known as a breaking hand because drawing a card is likely to "break" or "bust" you (cause your hand to go over 21).

2. When a dealer shows a 2 through 6, he is considered to be in a "breaking" position.

Breaking hands are when you and the dealer are weakest. These hands cause people the most trouble. In casinos throughout the world, the majority of people don't know how to handle breaking hands.

If you learn how to master the breaking hand, you will improve your Blackjack play about 25–30%.

When I teach Blackjack, much time is spent strengthening a player's strategy when confronted with a breaking hand.

Before tackling details of the various moves, you should understand two basic concepts:

1. When both you and the dealer are in a breaking position, let him do the hitting!

2. When the dealer is in a standing position (his up card is 7 through Ace) and you have a breaking hand, you *must* hit. Don't allow him to turn over his hole card and beat you without drawing!

That is it in a nutshell. But the casinos clean up in these situations because most novices are scared to hit breaking hands for the reason that they usually go broke! That's right, you can expect to go broke and lose often when you hit a breaking hand.

But, there will be times you don't break and you will improve your hand. Then, your chances of beating the dealer are a lot better. You won't have any of those chances if you don't hit. Believe me, when you have a breaking hand and the dealer shows a high card, you lose more hands by not hitting than you do by taking a hit.

I will give you a simple example which should help to destroy forever your desire to stand with a breaking hand when the dealer is in a standing position (remember, that means he's showing a 7 through an Ace).

Assume you have a 7 and an 8 (a total of 15) and the dealer is showing a Queen. You are afraid to hit because there is the possibility of breaking. Well, that is the biggest mistake you can make at the Blackjack table. If you stand, the burden of drawing is shifted to the dealer, after he turns over his hidden card. Since the card he turns over can only be one of thirteen different ones, look at each one individually to judge what would happen if you didn't take a hit. Of course, if you hit, the results won't be the same.

If the dealer turns over . . .

    Ace—He has Blackjack and you lose
    King—He has 20 and you lose
  Queen—He has 20 and you lose
    Jack—He has 20 and you lose
      10—He has 20 and you lose
       9—He has 19 and you lose
       8—He has 18 and you lose
       7—He has 17 and you lose
       6—He has 16 and a 38% chance of getting 17 or better
       5—He has 15 and a 41% chance of getting 17 or better
       4—He has 14 and a 44% chance of getting 17 or better
       3—He has 13 and a 48% chance of getting 17 or better
       2—He has 12 and a 51% chance of getting 17 or better

So, if you don't hit your breaking hand when the dealer shows a face card or a 10, you can expect to lose eight out of every thirteen hands. Even with the other five hands, when he doesn't beat you outright, he still has about a 45% chance of beating you when he takes a hit.

When you have a breaking hand and the dealer is in a standing position, don't hesitate—*Hit*!! If you lose, go on to the next hand. Don't worry about it; you made the right move.

If you have 12 and the dealer shows either a 2 or a 3, that's the only time you should hit a breaking hand when the dealer is in a breaking position.

If that strategy sounds peculiar, you can easily analyze it in the following manner:

As I explained in previous chapters, the dealer is weak when he has a 2 or 3 showing. But I also said you should respect him. He has ample leeway to draw a standing hand, no matter what his hidden card is.

Consider this when you hit 12: There are fifty-two cards in a deck. Sixteen ten-value cards will break you; the other thirty-six cards won't. You have odds of 2¼-1 of not breaking that 12 when you hit it. And, since you don't want to sit there and watch the dealer draw out on you, don't be afraid to hit. The odds are in your favor that you won't break.

If you have 12 and the dealer has a 2 or 3 showing, call for a hit.

Suppose you draw an Ace for a total of 13. Refer back to the Basic Strategy chart and you will see that 13 stands against a 2 or 3. (Always revert to Basic Strategy after you hit your hand.)

This is extremely important: Never deviate from Basic Strategy unless you are a card counter.

BASIC STRATEGY
WHEN YOU HAVE A BREAKING HAND

DEALER'S UP CARD	YOU SHOULD
2–6	STAND
7–Ace	HIT

EXCEPTION: WHEN YOU HAVE TWELVE

2, 3	HIT

KNOWLEDGE OF THE GAME

13

Weak Hands: Seventeen– Eighteen

This will be short and sweet. You already know the average winning hand is 18½.

When you have 17, you have zero! Eighteen isn't much better.

What can you do with your 17's and 18's? Nothing. You can't hit them, and they are almost worthless in certain situations.

When I am playing Blackjack and get dealt an 18, and the dealer has a 9 or higher showing, I expect to lose. If I lose, I forget about it and concentrate on the next hand. If I win, I'm happy I got the bonus. But, I still concentrate on the next hand.

When a hand is over, it's dead! Don't fret about past hands you lost. And don't waste very much time patting yourself on the back for a hand you won.

Think only about the present. If your mind is occupied with ancient history, you might not be aware of current events going on right in front of you. As long as you make the correct moves according to Basic Strategy, you've done all you can do. You gave it your best shot. Sometimes you'll win; sometimes you'll lose. Not even a 20 hand wins every time.

KNOWLEDGE OF THE GAME

14

The Soft Hands

I have already touched on soft hands and exactly what is meant by the term. To refresh your memory, a soft hand is any hand that contains an Ace—except when it is combined with a 10, Jack, queen, or King. Then, it is a Blackjack.

Realize how powerful you are when an Ace is one of your first two cards. The flexibility of using that card as either an 11 or 1, is tremendously strong. No three-card total can break you.

As soon as you see an Ace—if it's in your hand, you are strong—if it's the dealer's up card, he is strong.

In Atlantic City, you have the option of doubling your bet after any combination of two cards, so don't miss opportunities to double down on soft hands.

It is important to repeat the real reason for doubling your bet with any hand, even soft hands: *You don't double to improve your hand, you double to increase the amount of money bet against the dealer when he is in trouble.* Basic Strategy shows doubling with soft hands against the dealer's 3, 4, 5, and 6. It is a chancy move, but there is a slight percentage in your favor when you do so. Hence, I strongly recommend that you adhere to what the chart tells you to do.

It is so important to "get" the dealer when he shows his weak cards. And although the probability of getting a 19 or better with any of the six soft hands you would double down with is only three out of thirteen times (23%), you still have the opportunity of doubling your winnings when the dealer busts on his breaking hands.

You may have trouble memorizing these soft moves, but

take your time and the logic will eventually come to you. Remember, you want to get at least nineteen.

Suppose you have an Ace with:

2—You are looking for 8, 7, or 6
3—You are looking for 7, 6, or 5
4—You are looking for 6, 5, or 4
5—You are looking for 5, 4, or 3
6—You are looking for 4, 3, or 2
7—You are looking for 3, 2, or Ace

That's right, double down with a soft 18, an Ace and a 7. Your prospects for improving your hand is as slight as for the other five soft hands, but I still say to make the move. You already know how frail 18 can be.

Watch the Ace-7 versus power up cards (9 or higher). In these cases, the Basic Strategy chart says to hit—*not double down*! It is the old story of 18 being too weak, and the dealer's card being too strong.

Julian Braun points out in his computations, that you'll lose fifty-nine hands out of one hundred if you stay with the soft eighteen against a dealer's 10. He further states that if you hit the soft 18 against the dealer's 10, you will lose fifty-seven hands out of 100. Therefore, the percentage move is to hit rather than stand.

I know this is a difficult move to make, especially when you have a large bet riding on the play. But, if you want to play winning Blackjack, you'll have to learn to make the right moves. Not just once in awhile, but all the time.

The final two combinations have to do with Ace-8 and Ace-9. I have seen many people double down with these hands, and I cringe!

They are taking 19's and 20's and toying with them. When you reach 19 or better, either hard or soft, learn to stand. You will win most of the time.

Perfecting the soft hands will make you a tough player. Don't be discouraged if you get poor hits. It's not a good hand you're trying for, it's a winning hand. How can a winning hand be anything but a good hand? Well, a winning hand is one that beats the dealer. And, when the dealer busts, if you're still in the game, you have a winning hand. It doesn't matter if you have 20 or a pair of deuces.

In summary, the percentage of times you will reach 19 by drawing a card to soft hands is very small. But, whenever Basic Strategy tells you to increase your bet against the dealer when he is in a breaking position, don't be timid. He'll lose more when he is in trouble and you'll be able to increase your winnings. That should be your sole purpose for playing Blackjack.

KNOWLEDGE OF THE GAME

15

Soft Nineteen and Twenty

Soft 19 is an Ace and an 8. Soft 20 is an Ace and a 9.

I can't draw you 19 or 20 pictures to put my point across—you'll just have to pay attention: soft 19's and 20's are beautiful hands! I'd love to have them all day long, every day of the year. So, why do people double down with these hands? Beats me.

Actually, it doesn't beat me, it beats them! Which is the inevitable outcome of any stupid move. You'll get beaten in the long run.

If you are dealt a soft 19 or 20, don't take a hit and don't double down. Cherish your good fortune. These are great hands. Leave them alone.

When I see people in casinos doubling down with these powerful hands against the dealer's 5 or 6, I guess they are looking for extra money when the dealer's in trouble.

They're too ambitious! It's true you should double down against the dealer when he's in trouble, but only when you have poor hands to begin with. Never double down with a good hand. Be thankful you got it!

Keep these strong hands and build your winnings.

KNOWLEDGE OF THE GAME

16

A Pair of Aces

You're not seeing things, when you look at my chart and I tell you to split Aces only against 3 through 8, and hit against 9 through Ace, and the 2!!

I expect a lot of arguments from Blackjack players, who, for years, have split Aces regardless of what card the dealer shows.

Well, I justify not splitting Aces against 9 through Ace for the same reason I mentioned in Chapter Eleven that you shouldn't double down an 11 against 9 through Ace. With two Aces, you are even more powerful because you're more flexible. You are almost guaranteed to get a standing hand when you hit.

If you are still convinced that you would rather split Aces across the board, you haven't yet fully appreciated how strong the dealer is when he shows 9 through Ace.

Remember, you receive only one card on each Ace after splitting. Against power cards, be prepared to catch a big share of little cards—2 through 7, or Ace. With them, you'll wind up with weak hands. Then the dealer has numerous ways to beat you for twice the amount of your original bet.

By splitting Aces, the odds are that you'll end up with less than an average hand seven out of 13 times. What about the dealer's prospects when he has a 10 up? Well, he'll turn over a 9, another 10, a face card, or an Ace an average of six out of thirteen times—*and destroy you*!

I have spent hours and hours discussing this move with several professional card players. You would be surprised at how many of them are coming over to my theory on this hand.

An important part of learning how to gamble is to acquire or develop a theory of play that you can believe in and support. No single opinion is gospel. When you perfect this game, your theory on any questionable move is as strong as anyone else's. Nobody is actually wrong; it is merely different opinions on how to play different hands.

Before condemning my conservative style of play, try a six-deck shoe and run off a few hours of play using different tactics with a pair of Aces. Realize how powerful you are with two Aces to maneuver with

BASIC STRATEGY WHEN YOU HAVE TWO ACES

DEALER'S UP CARD	YOU SHOULD
3–8	SPLIT
2, 9–Ace	HIT

KNOWLEDGE OF THE GAME

17

Splitting Hands: 2's and 3's

You split a hand for the same reason you double down: When the dealer is in trouble, you want to get as much money bet against him as the law allows. One way to increase your original bet is by splitting.

Knowing when to split is vital to Blackjack strategy. I see people split 6's against a 10, and 5's against an 8, and an assortment of other totally illogical moves. The most illogical thing of all is for someone to play Blackjack who is not perfect at the game.

To begin with, a great many casinos allow splitting any two cards of equal value if they are dealt to you as your first two cards.

If you learn how to take advantage of this rule, it can be tremendously profitable!

I start by explaining when you should split 2's and 3's. This move is made whenever the dealer shows as his up card anything from a 2 through a 7.

Remember, the weak cards of the dealer are those from the 2 through the 7. If, for instance, you are dealt two 3's against the dealer's 7, look at the following chart to see what could happen if you don't split 3's, and instead call for a hit.

You have two 3's for a total of 6 . . .

YOU DRAW	YOUR NEW TOTAL
Ace	soft 17
2	8
3	9
4	10
5	11

6	12
7	13
8	14
9	15
10	16
Jack	16
Queen	16
King	16

Only three times do you get a decent hand of 9, 10, or 11, to allow you an additional hit and another attempt at getting 19 or better.

Eight times you will receive a breaking hand of 12 through 16.

One other time you will have an unappealing soft seventeen.

That adds up to nine out of thirteen times when you are vulnerable.

But, by splitting these same 3's when he has only a 2 through a 7, you are able to accomplish your primary objective of betting extra money against the dealer when he is in a weakened position.

When you draw to a single 2 or 3, there are at least three ways to achieve a double down situation.

For example, if you split 2's against a 5 . . .

YOU DRAW	YOUR NEW TOTAL
9	11, and you can double
8	10, and you can double
7	9, and you can double
6	8, and you can double
Ace	Soft 13, and you can double

This demonstrates where the player, by splitting 2's, has five chances out of thirteen to draw a card that allows doubling down against the dealer's weak up card of 5.

Imagine you start with a $10 bet and are dealt a pair of 2's against the dealer's 5. You split the 2's, and draw an Ace to the first 2 and a 6 to the second. Since the rules in most casinos allow doubling down after a split, you would now have the opportunity to bet $40, rather than the original $10.

Work some examples on your own to become aware of the numerous possibilities to bet more money when the dealer is weak.

One thing to remember when you split your hand: When the extra cards are dealt, take care of the first hand and complete it before doing anything with the second hand. Don't delay the game or embarrass yourself by switching to the second hand prematurely.

BASIC STRATEGY WHEN YOU HAVE 2'S AND 3'S

DEALER'S UP CARD	YOU SHOULD
2–7	SPLIT
8–Ace	HIT

KNOWLEDGE OF THE GAME

18

Splitting 4's

The chart shows that the only time you split 4's is against the dealer's weak 5 or 6. That makes sense.

Why would you want to split 4's against the dealer's 3? Too many cards will put you in a breaking position. Besides, drawing to 8 is not a bad assignment. Six cards (9 through Ace) will put you in a standing position with the dealer in a breaking position. Plus, two other cards (2 or 3) will give you a total of 10 or 11 for a better hand to draw to. That means eight out of thirteen cards will leave you in good shape.

You may wonder about splitting two 4's against the dealer's 4. It's a move than can provoke hours of discussion, pro and con. Card counters particularly like it when the deck is rich. Whichever way you decide to play, you are neither wrong nor right.

BASIC STRATEGY WHEN YOU HAVE TWO 4'S	
DEALER'S UP CARD	YOU SHOULD
5, 6	SPLIT
2–3, 7–Ace	HIT
4	HIT or SPLIT

KNOWLEDGE OF THE GAME

19

A Pair of 5's

You veteran Blackjack players won't like this chapter, but before you have a heart attack over it, first digest the contents.

You know I tell you to double down a 10 against the dealer's up card of 3 through 7 and that applies to 2-8, 3-7, 4-6, but not 5-5.

First off, test your memory bank and give me the answer to this question: "Why do you double and split?"

In case you have a memory lapse, the answer is: "To get more money against the dealer when he's in trouble." Stop!!!

Re-read that sentence until you fully understand why you double and split. Not to get a good hand, although you surely hope for that to happen, but mostly to get a lot of bread against the dealer when he's in trouble.

He's in trouble when he shows a 5 or 6 as his up card. OK, so if you double your 10 against the dealer's weak card of 5 or 6, you are doubling your bet when he's bobbing and weaving. But in Atlantic City where you can double after a split, here's what I want you to do:

Say you're betting $5 and the dealer's up card is a 6 while you are dealt 5-5. Simply slide another nickle on the board and say: "Split." Now if you get a 3-4-5-6 or ace, you have the opportunity of putting another $5 chip out there and doubling down.

Now you have $15 against the dealer. He swings over to the other hand of 5 and the same opportunity arises. You have a chance of getting $20 against the dealer rather than $10.

If you don't get him when he's in trouble, he'll kill you when he shows a power card, so strike while you can.

Before you condemn this action, go over it again. The Theory has merit. Naturally, in Las Vegas and other casinos that do not allow doubling after a split, you'd simply double all 10's against the dealer's 3 through 7. You'd hit against the 2 and 8 through Ace. In Atlantic City:

BASIC STRATEGY WHEN YOU HAVE TWO 5'S

DEALER'S UP CARD	YOU SHOULD
5–6	SPLIT
2, 8–Ace	HIT
3, 4, 7	DOUBLE

KNOWLEDGE OF THE GAME

20

Splitting 6's

Again, you face some obvious decisions. If you have been dealt two 6's, you are in a breaking position. Plain and simple. There are possibilities of drawing a 10, Jack, Queen, or King, and breaking.

You don't want that, so you split up the 6's. Agreed, drawing to a 6 is not as nice as kissing Miss America, but it's more cheerful than a broken leg.

I tell you to split 6's only when the dealer's up card is 2 through 6. He's in a breaking position, so you know he has to take a hit. Splitting 6's serves a double purpose: It allows you to avoid drawing to the breaking hand of 12, and it further gives you the opportunity to double your bet against the dealer when he is weak.

If the dealer's up card is 7 through Ace, take a hit. By now, the reason for hitting should be obvious.

BASIC STRATEGY WHEN YOU HAVE TWO 6'S

DEALER'S UP CARD	YOU SHOULD
2–6	SPLIT
7–Ace	HIT

KNOWLEDGE OF THE GAME

21

Splitting 7's

When you are dealt two 7's, split when the dealer shows 2 through 7. The reason for splitting is to avoid hitting a breaking hand. Sound familiar? It should. I just finished driving that point home in the last chapter. But 7's, unlike 6's, should also be split when the dealer shows a 7.

Why? Well, as I've mentioned before, 7 is a fairly weak up card. If you separate your 7's and draw one card to each, hypothetically you have two hands which are individually no worse than his lone 7 with another card. On an average, you should tie him. Wouldn't you prefer this situation to hitting 14? Don't lose the advantage of having two improved hands with twice the money bet against the dealer's 7!

A final warning: *Never, never* split 7's when the dealer shows 8 through Ace.

BASIC STRATEGY WHEN YOU HAVE TWO 7'S

DEALER'S UP CARD	YOU SHOULD
2–7	SPLIT
8–Ace	HIT

KNOWLEDGE OF THE GAME

22

Splitting 8's

I'm sick of hearing that crap about "you always split aces and eights." Baloney!!

My chart clearly states you do *NOT* split 8's against the dealer's power cards of 9, 10, Jack, Queen, King, or Ace.

This move will be contested by all the computer experts who claim that in nine million hands, you have a percentage factor in favor of splitting those eights.

Well, you aren't going to live long enough for two 8's to beat the dealer's power card, so the example I am showing you is based on trying to cut down losses, which is one of the keys to gambling sensibly.

Let's say you're betting $5 and are dealt two 8's against the dealer's King. If you put another $5 chip on the table, that dealer will split those 8's and give you two hands to play.

You'll get another card to go with each 8, but take a second to look at the reality of that move. I realize the cards will be dealt face up, but for the sake of example, let's say you are given the card face down.

Now the dealer has a King with a (down) card and you have 8 with a (down) card. And you have it twice.

What would you rather have? King with a card or 8 with a card?

Out of one hundred people giving the answer, ninety-eight will say, "naturally I'd rather have King with a card," and they'd be right.

One guy named P. Weebrane will say, "I dunno, it don't matter." So his answer doesn't matter.

Another friend of mine, I. M. Madork, will answer, "I'd

rather have the eight with a card" and sit there with that stupid grin on his face, looking both ways for a trolley to come. So his answer doesn't count.

Of course you'd rather have King with a card, over 8 with a card. Then why would you take a rotten hand of two 8's where you were risking $5 and turn it into two rotten hands where you are risking $10?

The answer is—you don't. You should hit that lousy 16, probably get beat, but the loss is one unit, rather than take two bad hands with a chance of losing twice as much.

So when you get dealt two 8's the decision isn't hard at all:

DEALER UP CARD	DECISION
2–8	SPLIT
9–Ace	HIT

KNOWLEDGE OF THE GAME

23

Splitting 9's

By splitting 9's when the dealer has a weak card up, you are putting yourself in an enviable position.

I've already explained why 18 is a mediocre hand. So if you have the opportunity to divide this hand and bet more money against the dealer when he is weak, *do it*!!

You split when the dealer shows 2 through 6, 8 or 9. Stand with he has 7, or 10 through ace.

Resist temptation and don't split 9's against the dealer's 7. If you don't split, you can expect the dealer to turn:

Ace for 18. You tie.

10 through King for 17. You win.

2 through 9 for under 17. He *must* hit!

Notice that there is no single card the dealer can turn over and beat you.

BASIC STRATEGY WHEN YOU HAVE TWO 9'S

DEALER'S UP CARD	YOU SHOULD
2–6, 8, 9	SPLIT
7, 10–Ace	STAND

KNOWLEDGE OF THE GAME

24

Splitting 10's

Last but not least among pairs, and the pros and cons of splitting them, are the 10's. I have one thought to pass along to you: *Never, never split 10's under any circumstances*! Period.

This isn't open to discussion, either by card counters or mind readers.

I've heard that certain Blackjack books say there are times when you should split 10's. Baloney!! I know of no card counters who practice this move.

When you have two 10's, you're in great shape. You're almost a cinch to win the hand. In fact, you can be darned sure of winning approximately 83% of the time. That's five out of 6 hands. Terrific odds.

Do you want to clear a table of good Blackjack players in a hurry? Split 10's. It is probably considered the most foolish move in the casino and good players will run from a table when somebody does it.

BASIC STRATEGY WHEN YOU HAVE TWO 10'S

DEALER'S UP CARD	YOU SHOULD
Any Card	STAND!

KNOWLEDGE OF THE GAME

25

Insurance

My phone rings off the hook with questions about Insurance. This chapter tries to answer most of them.

Insurance is a proposition bet that is allowed only when the dealer shows an Ace as his up card. As soon as the dealer finishes giving all players their first two cards, if he has an Ace showing, he will ask if anyone wants Insurance.

Since Insurance is offered only when the dealer is showing an Ace, you might think that it has something to do with a Blackjack. If so, you're right.

You can insure your hand against the possibility of the dealer having been dealt Blackjack. You insure your hand by placing a bet equal to half your original bet next to your cards in the part of the layout marked *INSURANCE*.

Suppose you're betting $10 and are dealt a 9, 10 (19). The dealer has an Ace showing and you wish to insure your hand. You place a $5 chip (half your bet) in front of you and wait. If the dealer turns over a 7, he now has a soft 18. He pays you $10 for your original bet because your 19 beats his 18, but he takes the $5 chip because he did not have Blackjack.

If he turns over a Blackjack, it beats your 19, and he takes your $10 chip. But, since you insured your hand against him having a Blackjack, and since the rule calls for Insurance to pay 2–1, you receive $10 back. So, you break even on the hand.

Explaining the rule is easy. Explaining any Blackjack rule is easy because the game has no complicated rules. The hard part of playing the game is firming your play with solid theory.

Here is another valuable opportunity to add to the theory you have already acquired.

The so-called experts are divided when it comes to taking Insurance. Most of the hassle is when you are holding strong hands of 19 and 20.

When you are sitting with a Blackjack yourself, *always* take Insurance. You are guaranteed of winning an equal amount of whatever you bet.

Example: You are betting $10 and are dealt a Blackjack. The dealer has an Ace showing. If you do not take Insurance, and the dealer turns over Blackjack, it is a push. You are dealt the best hand possible, and end up with a tie. Nothing!

If you take Insurance by placing a $5 chip (half your bet) in front of you, one of two things can happen:

1. The dealer turns over a ten-count card and has Blackjack. Your Blackjack results in a push (a tie) and you win nothing for your original bet. But, since Insurance pays 2-1, and you had Insurance, the dealer pays you $10, which is your profit for the hand.

2. If the dealer does not turn over a ten-count card, but, instead turns over a 9 (for example), he takes your $5 Insurance bet. However, you don't have a net loss of $5 for the hand because your Blackjack beats his soft 20 and he must pay you 3-2 for a $15 payoff. So, despite losing the $5 Insurance bet, you receive a $10 net profit.

Remember, if you have Blackjack and the dealer shows an Ace, *always take Insurance*. You are guaranteed a profit equal to your original bet every time!

The explanation of percentages for any other hands, including 19's and 20's, are too time consuming. It would be impractical for the little knowledge you would gain from it. There are many theories on why a player should or should not take Insurance with hands other than Blackjack, and nearly all of them are worthless.

Most professional gamblers take Insurance only when they have Blackjack. No other time.

Never, *never* insure weak hands (less than 19). The probability of the dealer not having a Blackjack and of your winning these sloppy hands is too great to risk the "premium" for Insurance.

A card counter knows the richness or poorness of a particular shoe, and just what percentage of picture cards are left. He is able to adjust his play accordingly. The neutral player does not have the advantage of being able to count cards and must play all hands as if the shoe is neutral. If you're not a card counter, then you are a neutral player.

My advice to neutral players: When you have Blackjack, take Insurance. When you don't, *don't*!!

KNOWLEDGE OF THE GAME

26

Re-Splitting

All casinos in Las Vegas allow splitting after a split. This is not so in Atlantic City. Those casinos offer doubling after a split, which interestingly is not allowed in most Las Vegas casinos at this time.

Suppose you were in Atlantic City and dealt a 4 against the dealer's up card of 6. By sliding another chip on the board, you can split the 4's. If the dealer gives you a 6 on that first 4, you put another chip in action and double that 10 against the dealer's 6.

You're getting maximum chips at risk when the dealer is bobbing and weaving, which is a key move.

But back up to where you split those 4's. Let's say you called for a double down bet, but the dealer gave you another four. Here's where re-splitting comes in, which is right now only allowed in Las Vegas.

Since the four was the same value as your split cards, you can now re-split again. You now have three hands of 4–4–4.

If another 4 shows, you can again put a chip up to signify an additional split hand. Keep in mind that some Las Vegas casinos only allow two extra splits, but that's a house rule that varies from place-to-place.

In any event, now you have four hands of which each is starting with a 4, and if your next card is an Ace, 5, 6, or 7 giving you soft 15, 9, 10, or 11, you may now double against the dealer's weak 6 in some places.

Re-splitting is a powerful tool, especially where you can double after a split and where you have Surrender. It allows you to get maximum money in play against the dealer's weak up card.

If a house allows re-splitting but no double after a split, go somewhere else. You'll find casinos that allow re-splitting and doubling after a re-split and Surrender.

That's where you should play.

KNOWLEDGE OF THE GAME

27

Practice Makes Perfect

Well, you have just digested another 25% of what you need to know to win at Blackjack. Knowledge of the Game! That, combined with Bankroll, which you studied earlier, means you're halfway home. But, you still need to master the principles of Money Management and Discipline.

From now on, with Knowledge of the Game, you should never again rely on gut feelings, wild guesses, or ESP when you play Blackjack.

Now, you must develop a practice schedule so you don't lose the knowledge you've gained. Every move should be second nature to you. Study the chart and practice until you are absolutely perfect with no hesitation:

Take two decks. Turn a card over on a table to signify the dealer's up card. Then expose two cards at a time. These represent the first two cards dealt to you in a succession of hands. Go as fast as you can and call out the correct move—hit, stand, double, or split—until you use up both decks. Do it over and over!

When you can call every move perfectly in forty-five seconds or less, you're ready for the real thing.

MONEY MANAGEMENT

1

What Is It?

Ever hear the term Money Management? You bet your sweet life you have!

Ever practice Money Management? You bet your sweet life you *haven't*!

Money Management is the third of the four indispensible steps toward the ultimate goal: Consistent winning.

Money Management! Everybody I speak to about gambling, asks about it. They are aware of its importance in gambling, yet never acquire a proper method of managing their money.

Money Management is the spoon that stirs the soup—that makes the meal complete. It ties together all of the loose ends of gambling, mixes them to a fine point and produces the end result.

I have already explained the part played by your Bankroll. You must have it just to walk into the casino. That is the first step.

Next, I gave you Knowledge of the Game. What moves do you make at the Blackjack table to increase your chances of winning? I taught you the best percentage move on every possible hand that can be dealt. Without this knowledge, you are wasting your time, because even with a heavy starting bankroll, the Vigorish will eat away at your money with each high percentage mistake!

A bankroll allows you to play. The knowledge allows you to play smart. What does money management do for you?

That's easy. It provides you with the correct plan for handling your bankroll. It is like a computer program—every move you make concerning money is predetermined.

With Knowledge of the Game, there are many instances where theory becomes a big part of a decision, especially with hands that can be affected by the richness or poorness of a deck. For instance two strong Blackjack players can have different theories about doubling down with a 5–3 (8) against the dealer's up card of 5. The percentage difference between doubling and not doubling is very close, and changes after the completion of each hand. So, valid theories among experienced players can vary.

Not so with Money Management. Your bankroll determines the amount you bet. And you must decide beforehand a win and loss percentage to tell you exactly when to leave a table.

If you can't manage your money, and refuse to learn how, you'll have absolutely no direction in a casino. You'll have no goal set for yourself; no idea of when to quit a table or even when to leave the casino for the day.

I won't say one part of the *BIG 4* is more important than the others. They're all too important and none can be ignored if you are to be a consistent winner. But I do know that more people lack Money Management than lack Knowledge of the Game.

People I speak with are widespread in their skill levels when it comes to playing Blackjack. Some are very good, some good, most poor. But there is a respectable percentage that has a fair knowledge of the game.

Money Management is a much different story. It's quite rare that I meet someone with a bona fide, dynamite method. Almost no one has a permanent system to follow.

When people come to my seminars, they take a test to determine their proficiency in Blackjack. Thousands of people have taken the test, which consists of twenty questions. The average number of wrong answers per test is about eight. That means people are 40% deficient in the Knowledge of the Game!

Isn't that unbelievable? 40%!!! Some have as many as sixteen wrong answers out of twenty. Any wonder the casinos report gross incomes of over $100 million every month?

Out of the thousands who have taken the test, only one got every answer right—one single, solitary person. A young lady.

A very pretty, articulate, young lady.

She arrived at an open house one night and said she knew the game of Blackjack, but wanted to know more.

She took the test and was perfect. Personally, I was happy to find someone who actually had it down pat. I remember her asking: "If I know as much about the game as you say I do, why do I usually lose??"

I told her: "You probably have no Money Management, and no discipline." She agreed that she didn't have either one.

She decided to learn Money Management. She also learned card counting. She is fabulous! Tremendous!

Her prior knowledge was helpful, but her desire to learn Blackjack, with Money Management and Discipline, makes her a great student of the game. She now plays in Atlantic City almost every Saturday. She's a $5 bettor with a $600 bankroll. Her winnings have exceeded $2,000.

You may not think $2,000 is a great amount of money, but don't tell her that. She has added the finishing touches to her game. She has Money Management and Discipline. She has learned how to win.

Then, there is this other guy. You may have sat next to him at a Blackjack table many times. He's having a great time—betting $15, then $50, then $100, then down to $35, and so on. He's joking with the dealers and pit bosses, needling other players good naturedly, and flirting with the cocktail waitresses. All in all, he's having a hell of a good time.

Watch out when he starts losing a lot! He gets nasty with everybody! What caused the downfall?

He had plenty of winning streaks, but didn't know how to take advantage of them. He bet heavily while losing and broke a lot of other rules.

He lacks Money Management. He has no game plan. He ends up losing his whole bankroll. It'll be a long ride home. Ever take it? Not much fun, is it?

Want to learn Money Management? Read on.

MONEY MANAGEMENT

2

Do You Want It?

I'm not too sure people want Money Management. This is not as ridiculous a statement as you might think. Like I said in the previous chapter, people readily admit that they don't have money management. And most of them say they are sorry they don't have it.

But how many are really willing to be restricted by it? Realize that Money Management is important, but the rules are tough to follow. The Discipline required to practice Money Management puts such a lid on most people's mode of play that they refuse to abide by it.

Look up the word *management* in the dictionary. It's control, discipline, restriction—things people hate to be imposed with. Especially when they're doing something "fun" like gambling. Do you consider it fun to give your money away? Well, that's what you'll be doing unless you know how to manage your money.

Most people undergo a personality change when they enter a casino. A guy who is too stingy to give his paperboy an occasional 25-cent tip for delivering his newspaper at seven o'clock every morning of the week suddenly becomes Mister Generous by handing $5 to a cocktail waitress he's never seen before for bringing him a complimentary glass of iced tea.

A boor who doesn't have the class to take his wife to a movie once a month, invites three strangers to dinner at the casino.

These people are out of control, so being confined by money management is out of the question.

How about the once-a-month visitor who takes a shot at the

tables with a $200 bankroll? Controlled betting? Forget it!

Every aspect of winning—each element of the *BIG 4*—demands some level of control:

Deciding what a proper Bankroll is, should be based on your own special circumstances. Waiting until you save that amount and then dividing it into three equal portions to finance three sessions.

Knowledge of the Game demands control on your part to practice and learn to respond automatically to each hand.

Discipline, which you still must acquire, is certainly a matter of control. The word describes behavior governed by strict rules of conduct. Controlled behavior!

Money Management is no different. It also requires control on your part. You must be willing to make all the sacrifices necessary to bring your game together.

Without Money Management, you can't be a consistent winner. There is no such thing as the *BIG 3*. It's the *BIG 4* or nothing!

MONEY MANAGEMENT

3

Where It Begins

In the Bankroll section, I touched a little on Money Management. The *BIG 4* is so tightly entwined—each part is so dependent on the other three—that the rules often overlap.

Where does Money Management begin? Before you enter the casino. Before the battle starts. While you're outside, you must make all of your decisions about winning, losing, and walking.

Assume you brought $600 to gamble with. Before you walk into the casino, decide what winning amount you will accept. You set the amount at 20% of your bankroll—or $120. That is the amount you will settle for on this trip. It doesn't mean that $120 is your win limit; it is your win goal.

Knowing that you will accept $120 as your profit for the day, you enter the casino and head for the Blackjack tables. You check until you find a table where the trend is in your favor. You take out $200 and grab a seat.

When you sit down, the $200 represents one third of your bankroll. It is called a session. Every bankroll is broken down into three equal sessions. The reason for doing this is to avoid the chance of losing too much money at one table.

It is essential for you to have a known Win Goal before you sit down at a table. But it is just as important to have a Loss Limit. A Loss Limit is the maximum you will let the house take from you before you call it quits at a table.

I'm sure you have seen people play down to their final chip. They refuse to leave until everything is gone!

Never, ever play down to your final chip! Never. There is no reason to. Set your loss limit at 40% of your starting session money. So, 20% is your Win Goal, and 40% is your Loss Limit. For each $200 session that becomes $40 as a Win Goal and $80 as a Loss Limit.

You can play comfortably at the first table, knowing that you still have two-thirds of your money safely tucked away. And $40 is the amount you would like to clear at this first table. Naturally, you would like much, much more, but you must learn to set a goal that you can easily reach.

The following chart breaks down your bankroll into sessions and shows you the correct table to play.

BANKROLL	PER SESSION	TABLE MINIMUM
$270	$90	$3
$360	$120	$3
$450	$150	$5
$600	$200	$5
$900	$300	$10
$2,250	$750	$25
$9,000	$3,000	$100

This chart tells you what table you are allowed to sit at. It doesn't know, and it doesn't care which table you *want* to play at! Don't grab a seat at a table with a higher minimum than you can afford—and you can only afford what your bankroll qualifies you for. Think of it as buying an airline ticket. If first class is too expensive, you sit in the coach section.

Entries for the $3 table are the absolute minimum you can have ($90 per session) and the preferred minimum ($120 per session), based on $30 \times$ and $40 \times$ formulas. For each of the other tables, the amount shown is the absolute minimum permitted per session.

The reason for the set number of plays is so that you can play comfortably during a session. If you go into a game with a short stack of chips, you may be swayed into making bad Basic Strategy decisions.

I am always a conservative player, but I am never a timid player. The two are totally different animals.

The conservative player is like the leopard that is always on the lookout and ready to attack a weak or lame antelope (the dealer who shows a 5 or 6), but gives a wide berth to a healthy bull elephant (the dealer who shows a 9 or higher).

The timid player will starve to death because he eats carrion, and then only when he stumbles over it. The timid player wins when the dealer's hand dies of natural causes (he busts!), but hardly any other time.

I have seen hundreds of people start at a table with $20 and immediately be dealt a 6–5 (11) against the dealer's up card of 4. Obviously, the proper move is to double down. But since this person has a small buy-in, he is afraid to double his bet because he can only survive a few loses before his money will be gone. Rather than betting the right way and risking twice the money, he pulls back and blows the choice opportunity to pounce on the dealer when he has a weak up card. Sure, sometimes the dealer wins these contests, but statistics prove that most of the time he doesn't.

A player stupidly refrains from attacking the dealer when he has a 4, or 5, or 6—one of the few times he is very weak! Why is it with the proper bankroll that there is no hesitation to make the correct double down move?

You'd probably be surprised at how a small bankroll affects different players. One the other hand is the character with $500 who plants himself at the $25 table, figuring he has enough bread to offset any losing streak. Neither type understands Money Management.

You can't go to a $5 table until your starting bankroll reaches at least $450, which breaks down to $150 per session—or thirty times the amount of the table minimum. Again, the desirable starting figure at a $5 table is a $600 bankroll, and $200 per session.

The $10 table is off limits until you have the barest minimum of $900. This breaks down to $300 per session, with thirty plays at $10. The proper amount is a $1,200 bankroll, made up of three $400 sessions.

Are you ready for the $25 table? Not until you have saved up $2,250, you aren't. Better yet, wait until you have $3,000 for three $1,000 sessions.

Do you think someday you might want to play at a $100 table? Well, the minimum and preferred bankrolls you need to play in that league are $9,000 and $12,000, each of which would be divided into three equal sessions.

These amounts are not pulled out of the air. They are based on thousands of hours of study of people's performances in the game of Blackjack. Playing habits, patterns and trends, all become reasons for establishing these controls.

The Money Management segment of the *BIG 4* is so complex and demanding, that 95% of the people who gamble, either don't, can't, or won't practice it. They admit they don't have it.

Once you learn it, follow it. If you don't, can't, or won't, look for less expensive entertainment—because Blackjack is certainly not something for you to take seriously.

MONEY MANAGEMENT

4

What Is Its Purpose?

For the benefit of those who are new to gambling, here's a look at what Money Management is all about.

I've already stated that millions and millions of people bet every day. This means not only on casino games such as Blackjack, Craps, Baccarat, Roulette, and Slots—but there are wagers made on football, baseball, basketball, soccer, hockey. Horseraces, both flats and harness. Poker, gin rummy, high-low, bridge, pinochle. Lotteries, keno, bingo. The list goes on and on.

People love to gamble. They like to win. They need to win. They need money, so they gamble to try and get it. But they lack the *BIG 4*, so they continue to chase the elusive dream— the pie in the sky, the pot of gold at the end of the rainbow. I am not putting you down for wanting it, just criticizing the way you go about trying to get it.

You wouldn't chase a Cadillac with a tricycle would you? Or, go after a lion with a water pistol? Of course not. Then why look for big killings in gambling with the lack of a proper Bankroll, lack of Knowledge, lack of Money Management, and lack of Discipline?

You've already learned about the first two. Continue to concentrate on the third.

How do you manage your money? First of all, not everybody brings the same amount of money to a casino. However, you *must* have enough money to be able to stay in the game until a streak comes your way.

A lot of people can't do that. They get so caught up in the play, so anxious to bet, that they put most of their bankroll in action during their initial hour of gambling.

I have seen so many people come into a casino and bet high stakes right off the bat, trying for a quick killing. I'm not saying it can't happen, or doesn't happen every day. But the percentage of time that it does happen—that's what you're fighting.

These people who bet heavily when they first come to a Blackjack table, and run into a hot dealer, drop so much of their initial bankroll, that the climb back is hard.

To prevent a disastrous early loss is the main reason behind the first rule of Money Management, which is to split your money into sessions. This helps you avoid getting wiped out early.

This allows you to stay in the game. It restricts your play at any session to one third of your bankroll, but still leaves you plenty of money to go to another game, if you lose at a certain table.

When you become perfect at Basic Strategy, you must next learn how to control or manage the money you play with.

Every bet you make must be based on the previous bet, whether winning or losing. It has absolutely nothing to do with hunches, feelings, or assumptions. A card counter bets according to the richness or poorness of each deck, or shoe. But the everyday Blackjack player, armed with Basic Strategy, must bet according to a predetermined pattern.

The better you manage your money, the longer you can stay in a game.

Do you know what a *chopping table* is? That's the common situation where the player and dealer win back and forth. You win, he wins, you win, he wins, for a series of hands. Do you know that there is a way to manage your money so that you will come out an automatic winner after one of these seemingly break even, give and take, sessions? Well, there is. And, it doesn't require you to vary your normal Money Management routine of betting.

If Money Management depended upon your knowing whether or not the dealer would win every other hand, it would succeed only for someone with occult powers—someone who can predict the future. Well, if you know what is going to happen the next hand, or every hand before it is played, you don't need to worry about Money Management. In fact, you don't need this book.

However, if the exact outcome of the next hand is unknown to you—if it's a mystery—then you need a Money Management system that works regardless of the pattern of wins and losses.

That's what I intend to teach you. It won't make you a winner every time. But, even when you lose, you'll lose less than you did before Money Management. You'll be alive to come back another day.

MONEY MANAGEMENT

5

Who Needs It?

Who needs Money Management? Everyone.

Every person, from the 50-cent daily lottery hopeful to the Arabian prince who nonchalantly shoves out $5,000 on each turn of the card in chemin de fer. They need it and so do all the people in between. And you need it.

No wager should be made without a strong, bona fide system in Money Management.

Casinos have been in operation a long time. They offer a fair operation, and it is your job to beat them. Forget about cheating. Casinos don't cheat. They don't have to cheat because people make so many stupid plays. This message is for all the crybabies who holler "cheat" after losing: *Casinos don't cheat!* Period!

I'll admit, they don't like the disciplined card counter, but that is because these few experts have learned how to swing percentages in their favor.

How many times have you been ahead in Blackjack, or some other game, and you didn't quit? Did you manage your bankroll to minimize your losses? Did you walk away with a profit after being ahead? If the answer is no, then *you* need Money Management.

MONEY MANAGEMENT

Blackjack Percentages

6

In the chapter on Vigorish, I explained the percentage you are bucking when playing Blackjack. Here is some more information on the subject:

So many people ask me what percentage they are fighting when they play in a casino. In Craps, everybody fights the same percentage, since each roll of the dice determines who wins and who loses all around the table. Everyone has the same chance of winning or losing. The percentages in dice remain constant, because the odds never change. For instance, the odds of making a 6 or 8 is always 6–5 against you. An hour ago, two hours from now, yesterday, today, a week from tomorrow, these odds will be the same.

But, in Blackjack, where decisions are made on each hand by each player, the richness or poorness of the deck changes the percentages for or against a player making a particular move. And, the percentages will be different each hand. So, card counters naturally have an advantage playing Blackjack. But, even if you are not a card counter and always make the right Basic Strategy moves based on a neutral deck, you're still better off than the haphazard player.

If you are dealt a 6, 10 (16), and the dealer shows a 7, you will have to make a choice, based on a neutral deck. If you take a hit, you will lose an average of 70% of the time, or seventy hands out of one hundred.

If you stand pat on 16 versus the dealer's 7, you will lose an average of 74% of the time, or seventy-four hands out of 100.

You know immediately that you have a rotten hand with 16 versus the dealer's 7. He can turn over five cards (10, Jack,

Queen, King, Ace) and beat you. Losing 70% or 74% of the time is going to hurt either way, but you must take the lesser of the two losses. Naturally, you hit, since the percentages say you will save an extra four hands out of one hundred.

Basic Strategy players know this and make the intelligent moves. Others guess, and because their plays are unpredictable, so are the percentages.

Basic Strategy players making all the correct moves can reduce the house percentage to 1½–2%. This is as good as it gets without card counting.

The hunch player may guess right most of the time or not at all. It isn't likely that he will reduce the house's slight edge over the Basic Strategy player. Sometimes he may guess wrong and still win the hand. Great. That happens to someone every day. Yet, I would hate to base my winning or losing at Blackjack on gut feelings or hopes.

I would prefer to sit down and play Basic Strategy and fight a steady 2% disadvantage, at most.

A survey of 40,000 Blackjack players in Atlantic City produced some amazing statistics. A whopping 92% said they don't use Basic Strategy—just gut feelings!

Of the 8% who use Basic Strategy (which is 3,200 of the 40,000), only 2½% of that number follow it religiously. (2½% of 8% is .002—or .2%—or 2/10ths of 1%—of the 40,000 total.) Can you believe this? Only eighty people! Here is a small group of people aware of something that works and not even three out of a hundred of them use it all the time! That's as bad as being aware of a tax loophole and not taking it. It's downright unpatriotic! No, it's *worse* than that!!

The ones who know Basic Strategy but don't use it all the time, sometimes make different decisions based on feelings, or bankroll, or position at the table. In other words, they deviate when they get scared.

Now you should understand why casinos report incomes of millions of dollars a month.

Incidentally, there is one more figure released. It reports that of the 40,000 screened only half of one percent of one percent (.00005—or .005%) are perfect, professional card counters.

Not just self-proclaimed card counters, but experts. That breaks down to a microscopic two out of 40,000 Blackjack players. And yet, the casinos make all the rules to stop the expert card counter. If the losses of 39,998 can't provide restitution for the damage done by two players, the destruction must be severe!

Well, it's definitely enough to grab the attention of the casino bosses. But, don't overlook what the other seventy-eight dedicated Basic Strategy players achieve. And those that practice smart Money Management are ahead of the rest.

MONEY MANAGEMENT

7

The Play

If you play the game of Blackjack perfectly using Basic Strategy, the house will win fifty-one hands out of one hundred and you will win forty-nine. That's 2% in favor of the house. But, you can think of it as almost an even game.

Why, then, if blackjack is an even game, are so many people losing so much? One answer is Money Management—or the lack of it, to be precise.

The chapters on Discipline explain the proper timing for walking from a table. This section stresses how to bet.

I have devised a method of play whereby you can lose 50% of the time, and still win money! In fact, you can win as little as 43% of the hands and end up with a profit!!

The theory is extremely simple. It is based on a regression/ progression type of wager, rather than an ordinary straight progression method.

To demonstrate, imagine the cards falling according to probability and you win forty-nine hands and lose fifty-one.

If you bet $5 on every hand, there would be forty-nine wins for a plus of $245, and fifty-one losses for a minus of $255. After one hundred hands, you lose the Vigorish, or $10.

This is the edge the house always has hanging over you and me, and rightly so. The house provides the game and must be compensated for services rendered. Don't get uptight about the Vig. Just make sure you play at games having the least Vig against you.

Many people in casinos use the Martingale (or doubling) system. When they lose, they double their next bet. They expect to win eventually. The trouble with this idea, is that *eventually* and *now* are in two different time zones. You can lose two, three, four, or even ten consecutive bets—"now" bets—and "eventually" is still waiting to happen.

The Martingale system has destroyed more players than "Russian Roulette" (which should not be confused with the regular zero, double-zero casino brand of Roulette).

I hear people argue: "The dealer can't win forever." They are right. He can't win forever, but he doesn't have to win forever to beat you out of your bankroll.

Let him win only six hands in a row. That isn't very much. What would happen if you bet a measly $5 to start with and double each time you lose?

Your bets will be: $5, $10, $20, $40, $80, $160, $320.

Suppose you win the seventh bet. Well, you would receive $320, but you would have to subtract your previous losses ($5 + $10 + $20 + $40 + $80 + $160 = $315). So, $320 minus $315, leaves you with a $5 profit.

In fact, no matter which bet you win with the Martingale system, your profit will always be no more than the amount of your original bet.

In this case, it is $5.

Suppose you lose the seventh bet? The Martingale system of bet progression says you must double after every loss. Therefore, you must be $640.

Trouble is, there is a table limit. In this case, it is $500. So, what happens when you bet the table limit? You bet $500, but you have already lost $635. Even if you win, your net is a minus $135. It will take you twenty-seven wins to cancel out this one losing streak.

This is *not* Money Management.

This system looks good on paper, and works 95% of the time on your living room floor. But, when it comes to the stark reality of a casino, it falls apart.

If doubling after losing doesn't make sense, then the other popular theory must be right. You know the one I mean: Double after you win. "Play with the house's money." As I said before, it isn't the house's money. Once you win, the money is yours!

If you try this method with an alternate "he wins, you win" sequence, you will realize this tactic doesn't make you a long-term winner.

The possibility of winning any even proposition is exactly that—even! But, the odds against winning two in a row is 3-1. So, when your winnings are riding for that second consecutive win, realize you are fighting triple the odds of the first win! The probability against three straight wins is 7-1. That's heavy!

You can win a hand at $5, let it ride, lose, and be down $5. That means you played a game of Blackjack where the chances of winning are 50-50, and you won once, lost once, and are behind $5. The house won a hand, and lost a hand, and is ahead $5.

Did you ever stop and analyze this chopping effect of win, lose, win, lose? And you still lose? You win as many hands as the dealer, but he takes more money from you than you take from him.

It's rough to win at Blackjack. So, when you win a hand, and lose the next hand, it is important that you show a profit.

My betting method regresses after the first win. This guarantees a profit for that bet series.

The time you spend at a table is a session. The first time you bet after a loss is the beginning of a series. Each series continues as long as you win. If you lose, the series is over. So, a typical session usually includes several series.

If you win a hand, the series stays alive until you lose. It is how you manage your money during a series that determines whether you will win or lose.

There is another approach which presumes you and the house are even. Therefore, there should be occasional streaks in your favor, so you should be able to bet the same amount every hand and leave a table after a hot streak and make a profit. Mathematically, the chances of this happening are remote.

What you want to do is offset "chopping" and come away with a profit.

THE PLAY

Your first bet is two units ($10 if you're playing at a $5 table).

If you lose, bet $10 again.

Lose again, bet $10.

This continues for four hands. If you fail to start a winning series in four hands, you must leave the table. Your session is over. You have a hot dealer, or a cold shoe. Either way, don't fight it. Walk!

If you do win that first hand at $10, your series has begun. When the dealer pays you $10, pull back the $10 you started with—and an additional $5, which is your profit. You leave $5 on the table as your next bet. If you lose this $5 bet, you have already pulled back the $10 you started with, plus a $5 profit. A loss ends your series and you count your winnings.

You win a hand, lose a hand, and show a profit of $5. That means that while playing the casino to a standstill, you have emerged a winner!

You can sit at a chopping table all day long and be a winner.

Bet $10, win. Pull back $15. Bet $5 and lose. Your profit if $5 for the two hands. One series. Let this continue for seven series and you win seven hands and lose seven hands. Yet, you still show a profit of $35.

If you try betting the minimum and then letting your profit ride each time, after seven series, you will be in the hole $35.

The amount of the first bet in unimportant, just so long as it is higher than the minimum allowed at the table where you are playing. You always need the opportunity to drop down to the minimum.

This scheme of betting *almost* guarantees you will be a winner for a series.

When will you not win?

Suppose you win the first $10 bet. Now you have $20 in front of you. Draw back your original $10 bet and $5 of the win amount. Leave $5 for the next bet. Even if you lose, you are sure of a $5 profit. Maybe!

What if you are dealt two 7's and the dealer's up card is a 6? What do you do? You split the 7's, naturally. So, you place another $5 chip on the layout to indicate a split.

On the first 7, the dealer gives you a 4, for a total of 11. Now, you must double down. So, you push out another $5 chip. The dealer gives you a 3, and you shudder. Your first 7 ends up as a disgusting 14.

The dealer hits your second 7 with a 3 for a total of 10. Again, you double down against the dealer's 6. You place another chip on the layout. This time he gives you a 5 for a total of 15. You have dug into your session money for an additional $15 over your original $5 bet. You are now risking $20.

The dealer still has to draw to his up card of 6 and you feel pretty safe. He turns over his down card and it is an Ace, giving him a total of 17. You lose the $20 and the series is over. It is one of the rare times when you can win the first hand in a series and end up losing that series.

This occurs when there are double down and split opportunities. Even though losses are possible, don't deviate from Basic Strategy rules. Always double down and split when the situation calls for it. Even though you will occasionally lose when you double down or split, these are the best times to increase your long-term winnings.

I call this regression/progression the New York system because the bet numbers 2–1–2 are the same as New York City's telephone are code: 212.

Two chips, one chip, two chips. That's the secret to the beginning of a winning series. Remember it!

MONEY MANAGEMENT

8

Sessions

Suppose you have a $600 bankroll (a comfortable amount I recommend). You set 20%, or $120, as your win goal. You divide your bankroll into three sessions and head for the tables.

So, you place $200 on the table. The other $400 remains in your pocket, and absolutely, positively, never gets touched during the first session.

A session is never governed by a clock, or any arbitrary time limit. It is based strictly on winning and losing. From a losing standpoint, you will stay in this session until you lose 40% of your $200 ($80). This is your Loss Limit. You cannot exceed this amount.

When you lose about $60 or $70 of a $200 session, you should be looking to run. The 40% Loss Limit should give you time for a winning trend to set in. If it doesn't, leave the table. Don't fight losing trends.

There are a couple of danger signals to look for to know when to exit a session. Don't be embarrassed to cash in your chips and leave. Don't worry about what the dealer or pit boss or other players think. This is your own private war, and nobody is going to write a check to cover your losses if you lose.

If you lose the first four hands in a session, that session is over. Leave the table. If you lose three, win one, lose three, win one, lose three, win one—aren't you being given signs that the cards are not coming your way? Leave the session.

I have already told you how to key a table. You should never sit at a table until you take a reading on how that particular dealer is doing. Key his up cards for a period of ten hands. Compare the number of power cards (9 through Ace) with the weak cards he turns over.

I suggest no more than six power cards to four weak ones to allow you to compete at a table. If he turns over four or five straight weak cards, sit right down. He is in a down cycle.

As you become proficient at Blackjack, you will pick up your own theory of percentages, which allow you to play comfortably.

Once the preliminary keying is done and you take a seat, it is important that you constantly keep track of your money so you will not exceed the 40% loss limit. If the dealer has a hot streak and you can't seem to gain on him, it is OK to leave after losing only 25–30%.

Win goals can be very flexible because different players are satisfied with different amounts. Some players will accept a 10% win. Others want at least 15%. And others insist on 20%. If you want more than that, I suggest you lower your sights in the beginning.

Although your Win Goal may be conservative, never, never leave a table while you are in the middle of a hot streak, even if you surpass your goal.

I have been at a table where the dealer is ice cold and all of the players are winning and having a good old time. Suddenly, one player looks at his watch, sees that it is six o'clock and proclaims: "Time to eat!" He abruptly leaves the table to go fill his tummy.

Can you believe anything so crazy? As long as the dealer is cold, stay glued to your seat. Enjoy your good fortune while it lasts, because it certainly won't last forever.

Once in Las Vegas, when things were going in my favor, I remember playing poker for two and a half days—stopping only to walk around the block to stay awake, or going to the washroom to put cold water on my face.

When you are winning, the adrenalin keeps pumping and gives you the extra energy to stay in the game.

If you reach your Win Goal, there is nothing wrong with putting part of your winnings aside to assure yourself of a profit for the session. Play with the excess. If you lose that, leave the table. If you continue to win, pull some and "bury" it. Pull and play. Pull and play. Win $10; bury $5.

If the excess money dwindles, kill the session.

It is imperative that if you get ahead in a session, you must leave that table with a profit. Learn how to win. It will become contagious.

MONEY MANAGEMENT

9

The Series

Streaks are what separate winners from losers. And, a streak begins with the first win. Once you win your first hand, you are on your way.

There is no such thing as "due" to win or lose. The biggest failing of players in a casino is not capitalizing on hot streaks. They don't know they are in one until it's over. Then it's too late.

Some players reduce their bet when they think it is "time" to lose—and, increase their bet when they think it is "time" to win. Both ways ultimately lose.

What is a streak? Three or more wins in a row.

After the regression bet (bet number two), which practically assures a profit when you win the first bet in a series, you increase your bet each time you win.

Suppose $10 is the amount of your first bet, and you win. The next bet (your regression bet) is $5, and you win that one. Then you bet $10 again, letting the second bet "ride." Even if you lose this one, you still have a profit of $5 for the series.

If you win the third hand, you win $10. At this level, "up and pull" your bets, which means to go up one unit and pull back the difference for a profit.

Your fourth bet should be $15, which gives you another $5 profit. If you lose this hand, you are $10 ahead. If you win, you have a variety of options. You can:

1. Bet $20 and pull back $10, or
2. Bet $25 and pull back $5, or
3. Bet the same $15 and pull back $15, or
4. Bet $10 and pull back $20, or

5. Bet $5 and pull back $25.

The last two options are super conservative, but are not bad for new players. Learn to win!!!

There you have five variations of betting and you have just reached a level of three units. As the series continues, you will encounter more choices with each winning hand. You must be prepared to deal with each one without hesitating.

I suggest the basic play for the New York system to be: 2–1–2–3–3–4–5.

At a $5 table, that translates into the following bets: $10, $5, $10, $15, $15, $20, $25.

When you reach the $25 level, you have many options. But, I want you to consider only four:

1. Same bet ($25) and pull $25, or
2. Reduce the bet to $20 and pull $30, or
3. Bet $15 and pull $35, or
4. Go back to $10 and pull $40.

A series begins with a win and ends with a loss. A push keeps the series going. The size of your first bet depends on how much session money you have. But, the first bet must always be higher than the minimum, so that the second bet can be regressive.

Memorize the New York numbers: 2–1–2–3–3–4–5.

MONEY MANAGEMENT

10

Variations

As I pointed out, the number of variations of the New York system can be broken down into any number of categories, depending on the bankroll of each individual.

The basic idea, though, should never be changed. Just be sure you regress your second bet in a series (after a win), to take advantage of getting into a winning position.

Each person's own theory of betting will apply. Some may want to bet aggressively, while others will opt for a more conservative approach. Neither side is wrong. As you become more and more proficient in the game of Blackjack, you may want to increase your bets, because you will definitely minimize your losses, and have higher bankrolls with which to start.

However, in the beginning, I strongly urge you to bet small until you master the series that you will concentrate on.

There is plenty of time to go for the big wins. In the beginning, learn how to win.

I have broken down several variations of betting series, and one or more of these may appeal to you.

It is possible for you to come up with your own individual pattern.

Remember the basic rules:

1. The first bet at a table or session is called a series.
2. If you lose the first hand, that series is over, although it consists of only one hand.
3. Never lose more than the first four hands at a session. If you lose the first four hands, leave that table.
4. If you win the first hand in a series, regress your second bet.

5. If you lose a series, always revert back to an amount higher than the table minimum, but never higher than the first bet of the previous series.

6. When you lose 40% of your session money, that session is over. But, that doesn't mean that you have to stay at that table to lose the whole 40%. You can kill a session after you have lost 30%, and the dealer continues to turn over power cards.

7. After you win approximately 20% of the amount of your starting session money, divide your profit in half. Put one half aside, never to be touched again at that session. Play with the other half until it is finished.

8. After the split of your profit, if you continue to win, add one half of these winnings to your profit pile, and the balance remains in play with your excess.

Go over these rules repeatedly, until you have them memorized.

Variations at a $3 table. To be used with a $300 bankroll.

A	B	C	D	E	F
$5	$5	$6	$7	$7	$10
$3	$3	$3	$3	$3	$3
$6	$5	$7	$8	$7	$7
$9	$10	$10	$8	$10	$12
$9	$10	$10	$12	$15	$12
$12	$15	$15	$15	$15	$15
$15	$20	$20	$20	$20	$20

After reaching the $20 plateau, your options are:

1. Repeat $20 bet, or

2. Regress one $5 unit at a time, as you win, making the next $15, then $10, etc., or

3. Revert back to a $5 bet, and start progressive climb again.

(For the novice at the $3 table, I suggest the first option: *Repeat $20 bet*.)

Variations at a $5 table (bankroll $450).

A	B	C	D	E
$10	$10	$8	$7	$10
$5	$5	$5	$5	$5
$10	$10	$7	$9	$8
$10	$15	$10	$12	$12
$15	$15	$10	$15	$15
$20	$20	$15	$15	$15
$25	$25	$20	$20	$20

When you reach seven wins, the options are as shown previously. (At the $5 table, I would like to see you start at C.)

Variations at a $10 table ($900 starting bankroll).

A	B	C	D	E
$20	$20	$20	$25	$30
$10	$10	$10	$10	$10
$15	$15	$15	$15	$15
$15	$20	$15	$20	$20
$20	$20	$20	$20	$20
$25	$30	$30	$30	$30
$35	$40	$45	$40	$40

Again, the variations at this level are optional. (For the conservative person, begin with Column A.)

Let's go to the $25 table, where your starting bankroll should be $2,250.

A	B	C	D	E
$50	$50	$40	$40	$50
$25	$25	$25	$25	$25
$40	$30	$35	$30	$50
$40	$30	$35	$30	$50
$60	$50	$50	$45	$75
$75	$60	$60	$60	$100
$100	$75	$75	$75	$150

Your options can be more aggressive as you increase your series bets, but you must stay within the limits of your starting bankroll. If it calls for you to play at a $5 table, use the variations for that table.

The theory on this regression/progression type New York

system has so many options and variations, that too much space would be used, showing all of these breakdowns.

Naturally, not everyone goes into a casino with the same amount of money. The problem that hurts most, however, is that they try to win an amount in excess of the logical amount they should expect, based on their bankroll.

When you learn to play within the confines of your starting bankroll and session money, you will see a fantastic change in the consistency of your wins. They won't be large wins, necessarily, but then they will be more consistent, and when you do lose, the losses won't destroy you.

Work slowly into the category of betting big bucks by building a bankroll large enough to sustain you through the dry spells. Then, when you get into a red hot series of bets, you will be making heavy scores, and not betting scared money, or minimum amounts.

I have listed many variations of bets that could be used. Naturally, you could make your own progression formula, provided you regress the bet on the second hand (following a win), of any series.

As you become more proficient at the game, and at winning, you will find a more aggressive style creeping into your series formula.

Until then, start slow, bet conservatively, learn to win.

MONEY MANAGEMENT

11

Theory of Method

Remember what I said about gambling, many, many pages ago? Every move has a logical reason. Either it is based on percentages favoring it—or, the alternate decision, which is a gut decision, is so adverse to giving you a good chance of winning, that it shouldn't even be considered. The same is true of Money Management.

This game of Blackjack is considered an even game. By knowing Basic Strategy or correct percentage moves perfectly, you can reduce your chances of losing very close to only 50%, and that is putting you on a par with the house as to the possibility of winning as many hands as it does.

That's why Money Management becomes so important. If you sat at a Blackjack table, betting $5 on each hand, and won a hand, then lost the next hand, the result would be simply: You would win $5, lose $5, and would be even with the house.

If your system of betting called for you to win a hand, and then let the whole $10 ride on the next hand, the result would read: Win a hand, lose a hand, and lose $5. Doesn't the illogical result jab at your gut? Here you are playing the house exactly even. You have played two hands, and each side won once. Yet you are out $5. This could happen over a string of ten hands, with the wins and losses bouncing back and forth, and even if you were betting only $5 a hand, the five wins you made and the five losses you suffered would show a 50–50 split in decision, but a deficit of $25 to your bankroll.

This regression system protects against just such a pattern, and still allows you to win a large sum, as the streak progresses.

Study it and analyze the theory behind the procedure of betting. The win on the first hand, followed by reducing your second bet, assures you of a profit whether you win or lose the second hand.

Ninety-five percent of the people who play in casinos have absolutely no predetermined Money Management system. It is the "whole ball of wax" where gambling is concerned.

I want to slowly rehash the betting system that most people tend to stay with. It has no direction, and only keeps the player in the game long enough to be ground out of his bankroll.

Remember that Blackjack is almost an even game, when, and I repeat, when the player has perfected Basic Strategy.

By average, you should win just about as many hands as the dealer, and if you bet an equal amount of money on each hand, you are simply exchanging chips back and forth. Then, when the dealer runs off a string of six or seven wins in a row, you will begin chasing your lost money, increase your bets, forget the conservative manner you were following and, all in all, lose complete control of your game.

This is a weakness suffered by most novices, and many veteran players. Learn to set up a pattern of Money Management. In Blackjack, it is very hard to win four or five hands in a row, so settle on two or three wins. In fact, to change your entire approach to the game, we would like to see you settle for two wins in a row. I'm not saying that you can't have long winning streaks. I'm trying to condition you to winning. Accept small gains, and the big ones will happen.

It is so disheartening to sit at a table and watch some guy bet $10 and win, and let the whole $20 ride on the next hand. Again he wins, and now has $40. He figures that this is his run and pushes the whole $40 into play. He loses!!!

Simple arithmetic shows that he won two hands, lost one hand, and ended up down $10. That proves out as follows: Playing a game that, at best, is only a toss-up, you must make some profit out of each win. In this case, you won two out of three hands, for 67%, and ended up a loser.

Do you see the fallacy of always *letting it ride*?

I realize you follow the old adage: "If you don't shovel it in, you can't hit pay dirt."

That's all well and good. But someday you have to face up to the fact that winning consistently, in small amounts, has it all over the theory of constantly going for the kill. I will show you how to eventually go for the big score, but the first rule is "Learn how to win!"

To do that, you must understand the theory behind my method. Foremost is understanding how difficult it is to win at Blackjack. When you realize this, you will be able to accept small wins.

I, personally, sitting at a Blackjack table, feel very badly for other players in the game, who have absolutely no system of increasing or decreasing their bets after subsequent wins or losses.

I have already berated the method of simply sitting there and betting the same amount, hand after hand.

I have also discounted the method of winning a hand, and then letting it all ride on the next hand. It just defies true percentages.

Since we are calling Blackjack an even game, for the sake of example, just examine the odds against winning two hands in a row. It is 3-1 against you. That's why people continue to lose so often at gambling. They fail to understand the percentages working *against* them.

The regression system is based on winning one hand in a row. Once that is accomplished, everything else is gravy.

If your first bet is $10, and you win the hand, take the $10 you won, plus $5 off the board, and bet $5 on the next hand. Even if you lose that hand, you still have the $10 you initially laid out, plus a $5 profit. It is not uncommon to get into a win, lose, win, lose pattern at a table. Make those chopping situations pay off.

The theory is very basic. Once you win that first hand, your series has started. You then pull off your initial bet, in this case $10, and half of the $10 you won, namely $5. Right now, you are sitting pretty. In effect, the next hand is free. Win or lose, you cannot be out money after the hand is finished. You will be either ahead $5 (if you lose) or ahead $10 (if you win).

Basically, the object of this method is to take advantage of every single win that you have in the casino.

The amount of your first bet is not important, only the fact that your first wager is higher than the amount that you will regress back to.

In that way, you guarantee that even if this is only a small regression from your first bet to your second, assuming that the first hand wins, you will be assured of a profit for that series.

This chapter on theory is the full explanation of the New York system. It is basically a repeat of what I pointed out in prior chapters, but if you don't understand the theory of a move, then the results will make no sense.

Again I ask you, if you still don't completely grasp the reasoning behind the New York system, go over this chapter again, using chips as pawns, to fully gain the impact of this method.

MONEY MANAGEMENT 12

Regression Grasp

Stop right here. Don't go flying through this chapter until you zero in on the question that I'm going to hang on you:

"Did you grasp the total concept of the message that was laid out in the previous chapters?"

In layman's terms: Do you know what the heck I just explained to you??

Since some of your bought this book (although most of you were probably too cheap to lay out the money and just borrowed it), to learn how to win at Blackjack, the Regression Money Management method is far and away the key to that goal.

Again, I'll break down the explanation in order to make sure you all understand the concept:

This Regression Money Management method is the powerful tool that allows you to know exactly what your bet is after a win and exactly what your bet is after a loss.

The fact that you lock up a profit after the first win, by taking back your original bet plus a profit, puts you into the position of playing the house even and still showing a guaranteed profit.

I want to re-emphasize the theory and even if you think you've got it down pat, look at it one more time.

You're at a $5 table and your first bet is $10. It could be $6 or $7 or $8 or $9 or $12 or $15 or $20 or any amount higher than the minimum.

You win your $10 bet and the dealer slides two chips next to your original two-chip bet.

Immediately take back the $10 you started with, plus a $5

profit, and bet $5. Even if you lose that $5 bet, you've got a profit locked up for that Series.

The next chapter explains the method of "up and pull," but be sure you first grasp the Theory of the Regression. This is going to change your approach to gambling.

Just remember a few more points. If you lose the first three hands of a session, get out of there. If you predetermine four straight losses and it happens, ditto, get moving.

Also predetermine the amount of your starting series, based on a previous loss. You can make it any one of the following:

1. $10-$5-$10-$15-$15-$20
2. $10-$5-$10-$5-$10-$15
3. $10-$5-$8-$12-$10-$5
4. $10-$5-$7-$10-$12-$18
5. $8-$5-$8-$10-$15-$20
6. $7-$5-$7-$10-$15-$10
7. $6-$5-$7-$7-$10-$15

If you lose your first series bet of $10, drop to $8, if you lose, drop to $7, if you lose, drop to $6. If you lose, leave the table.

OK, if you've grasped the Theory of the Regression, you can move on. But if you haven't, go back and read those chapters again until you get this method engraved in your brain.

This is what Money Management is all about. And Money Management is what winning is all about.

MONEY MANAGEMENT

13

Up and Pull

This will be easy to understand, if you've truly understood the regression method. Just peek back at the various series that were laid out for you and notice that each one shows in a winning series you grabbing a profit after a win and increasing your next bet in most instances. Thus the term "up and pull." You are upping your bet and pulling back a profit.

In some cases, however, you bet the same amount, others you regress and others you increase or up your bet. But in every instance—except when betting the table minimum after regressing—you pulled back a profit.

My friend Imus Pressit, who believes that gambling is a constant succession of pressing your bet, is suddenly silent.

This dork, who never pulls back a profit, constantly reinvests every winning bet and leaves a bundle of chips at the mercy of the casino when a loss occurs. But he may be seeing the light.

Imus Pressit is just like most people who gamble. He doesn't realize that the key to winning is pulling back a profit after every winning hand, rather than banging away, going for the kill.

The Theory of Up and Pull isn't rough to understand. It lets you increase your bet but does not allow you to invest the whole amount.

The key word is "pull." It rhymes with "intelligence," so it should be easy for you to remember. (Yea, I know, you don't think it rhymes, but how would you know the difference—you don't even know how to gamble sensibly, so how can you claim to be a genius in English prose?)

Anyhow, at least grasp the message of "up and pull" and the important part of this move. You're grabbing a profit for every hand you win at the tables.

"It's not how much you win, it's how little you lose."

Go back over that last sentence and read it over and over and over and over and over and. . . .

MONEY MANAGEMENT

14

Guarantee and Excess

OK, you're deep into the Money Management part of this book and all of you should realize that this is the key part of your attempt to win at gambling.

Now we split the players into two groups: conservative and aggressive. There's no secret as to which direction. I lean—it's conservative—or rather, super conservative.

That doesn't make me right or wrong. It just means that I believe that the best way to handle gambling is to grind out consistent returns, regardless of the amount.

But some of you may like to play a more aggressive style. That's where this method of Guarantee and Excess comes in. Its purpose is to allow you to rat-hole a profit and still go for a large return.

Actually the method is very basic and you should be able to incorporate its theory into your scheme of play.

Naturally, the first thing you do is set your Win Goal. That's your primary concern, reaching that goal. When you do, the process of Guarantee and Excess is now put into play.

Take your Win goal and break it in half. Put your starting session money in your pocket. Put one half of your Win Goal in your pocket, leaving the other half on the table.

At that point you have salted away your starting session money and made sure that you will not suffer a loss at that session.

By splitting your Win Goal in half, you now have two stacks of chips. The half you put in your pocket is called your Guarantee. You are guaranteed to leave that table with your starting session money and a profit.

The amount of that profit is based on the amount of your starting session amount. If you had a large session amount, you'll have a nice profit as your Guarantee.

If you started with a small session amount, then the profit will be smaller but at least it's a profit. And that Guarantee can never be touched again. That's a *big, big* never. Period.

The other half of that Win Goal is called your Excess. You now can continue to play with that amount.

So what that it is not a big enormous amount of money. Even if you lose it, you have your Guarantee safely tucked away and anything you win with the Excess is simply extra money.

You can stay at that table as long as the Excess stays alive, and when it is gone, or when a portion of it is gone, whatever amount you set, then you can wrap up that session!

Guarantee and Excess are important parts of your Money Management plan, and they're easy to grasp:

1. When you reach your Win Goal, break that amount in half.
2. Rat-hole your starting session amount.
3. Rat-hole one half on that Win Goal, called your Guarantee
4. Play with the other half which is called Excess.

There you have the play, and you aggressive players can go for the jugular with the Excess.

In the next chapter, we'll go over the handling of the Excess but at least be sure you've got this method completely understood.

MONEY MANAGEMENT

15

Handling the Excess

Just because you've reached the Excess part of your Win Goal doesn't mean you start making stupid moves.

It's OK if you increase the amount of your series bets but once a series is complete, break the profit in half again, repeating the process of putting half with your Guarantee and half staying with the Excess.

Suppose your Win Goal resulted in a plus factor of $60. After socking $30 away, you begin your Excess with the other $30.

Every subsequent winning series in the Excess part of your play is then divided in half between the Guarantee and Excess.

This keeps increasing the amount of your sure-pot profit when you finally do leave that table and keeps increasing the amount of money you can play with.

Here again I emphasize that you are in control as to what series you set up, because I'm trying to allow you to become aggressive if you so desire.

I didn't say I was condoning it, but just making sure you realize I'm not condemning it.

The bottom line is that the Excess play should have you feeling comfortable, with that Guarantee making a nice nest egg in your jeans.

In my videos you'll see aggressive methods such as the Paroli, the 1-2-2, the 1-2-3, and the La Bouchere Systems. These methods allow you to step up your betting while still keeping a smart hold on your Discipline tactics.

One more reminder: Keep sticking profits in your pocket after either a winning hand or a winning Series.

They call that move Money Management.

In a nutshell, let me zero in on the handling of the Excess:

1. When you begin a session, set up the Win Goal.
2. When the Win Goal is reached, divide into Guarantee and Excess.
3. Half in your pocket is the Guarantee, along with all of the session amount.
4. The other half (Excess) allows you to get aggressive, while setting up plateaus of winning amounts.
5. As you reach these plateaus, you can escalate the size of your series.
6. Stay at that session as long as the Excess stays alive.
7. Keep dividing subsequent series wins into Guarantee and Excess.
8. When the Excess starts to drop, leave that session.
9. If you lose three straight hands in the Excess part of your play, leave that session.

There you have a look at the handling of the Excess part of your Win Goal. The amount of the series that you set can stay the same as when you started, or it can be increased. That decision is yours.

MONEY MANAGEMENT

16

Plateaus

Plateaus provide another control factor in the all important part of Money Management. Just concentrate on exactly what a plateau is.

They will be levels that you will set in series betting as you continue to win in a certain session.

Let's say you've finally landed at a table where the dealer is ice cold. Knowing how to take advantage of that obvious cold streak on his side will enable you to maximize your profits.

M. T. Hedd is a typical dope at a Blackjack table. He'll be in the throes of a hot streak, but instead of realizing it and taking advantage, he's all wrapped up in unimportant side tracks.

He's borrowing a cigarette from a friend, looking for the cocktail waitress, giving advice to the other players, checking out the blonde two tables over while using his other eye to see that his wife is not bearing down on his table, posing stupid questions to the dealer about where she has her nails done, pressuring the pit boss for a comp, and asking every other person who passes by what the football scores are.

In other words, he hasn't a clue as to whether that dealer is hot or cold.

As soon as you see the dealer go cold and you work your way into the Excess part of your Win Goal, start to set up plateaus, so as to know when you will increase your bets.

Start off with plateaus of $50 each for two levels. Then swing into $100 plateaus and then $150, etc.

As soon as your Excess begins, let's say you are using a series that reads $10-$5-$10-$15-$20-$25.

Set a plateau of $50 and when you reach it, increase your

133

series to $15-$5-$5-$10-$18-$20-$30.

The next plateau is again $50 and if that is reached, you go up to $20-$10-$15-$25-$35-$20-$30.

The plateau after that is $100, whereby your series goes to $20-$5-$10-$20-$30-$20-$25-$40.

The options are innumerable because you can be playing loose, freely aware that your Guarantee is climbing and you are taking advantage of your streak.

The use of plateaus keeps your mind glued to points where you can adjust your series to capitalize on your good fortune.

I know this might seem like I'm giving you a lot of things to do and you're right.

Why shouldn't you have all of these methods applied to your play? This is war, baby, and playing like M. T. Hedd is gonna have you blowing a lot of bread at tables where you should be making money.

Understand the power of the plateau and use it. You don't have to make drastic increases in your betting series, and in fact, I don't give a rat's tail if you keep it the same all the way through your session.

Just as long as you win and leave the casino with more than you started with.

Man, it's so nice to win. In fact, it's almost as good as getting into your car and finding that Miss World has parked her carcass on your front seat, or for you ladies, Mr. Universe.

Take that back—winning money isn't that good, but at least it's a great feeling.

Think I'll go out and check my car. Maybe I'm in a hot streak.

MONEY MANAGEMENT

17

Bad Trends

One of the most important parts of your day is finding a trend, in whatever game you play. In Blackjack, you are looking for a dealer who is going cold. Funny thing about trends is that no one seems able to explain why they occur, let alone know when they'll come.

But they do happen and the trick is to be able to take advantage of them. I know you can tell me when they're over, but I want to show you how to take advantage of them while they are happening.

Lee Tillate is always a day late and a dollar short. When he plays Blackjack, Lee Tillate is always a little late in reading a bad trend and that's almost as bad as not being able to take advantage of a hot streak.

By now you should understand that there are three types of trends:

1. Chopping Table
2. Hot Trend
3. Bad Trend

The dope who sits at a table and loses $200 out of a $300 starting bankroll is too stupid to realize he's in a losing streak and thinks his "luck" is due to change.

But there are no timetables in losing trends. They could last for hours and the bad players sit right at the same tables, pouring chip after chip down the drain.

Being able to zero in on a bad trend doesn't take the brains of a rocket scientist. If you lost three hands in a row, don't you think that's a big enough signal to get you to walk?

No, it usually isn't. I see guys lose six, seven, or eight hands in a row and still sit at that table, unaware that they're facing a scorching dealer.

Trends happen at every table, in every casino, all over the world. Understanding these trends and being able to cope with them will be the difference between winning and losing on a given day.

That's why I stress the importance of setting Loss Limits and Win Goals. Since I believe in holding down losses, I want you to first grasp the use of Loss Limits and the ability to recognize losing trends.

If you lose three hands in a row, you're in a bad trend. What's so hard about wrapping up that session and searching out a dealer in a cold streak?

Yet most players don't have the brains to do that. They continue to sit at that table getting whacked. They just don't understand trends.

The next chapter shows you how to handle hot trends and then we'll slide into charting.

But for now, get to thinking about cold trends. When you're losing:

1. Obey Loss Limits.
2. If you lose three or four in a row, leave that table.
3. If at a chopping table, leave as soon as a majority of hands result in a loss.
4. It's not necessary to play down to your Loss Limit.

If you're serious about winning at Blackjack, get to realize how important trends are.

You've just read about losing trends, let's swing over to hot (good) trends.

MONEY MANAGEMENT

18

Good Trends

Your day in the casino will be filled with trends, both good and bad. Trends dominate in gambling.

When you're in a rotten streak, the trick is to cut those losses and wrap up the session. The ability to read a cold streak will save you tons of money in your gambling forays.

Jack DeJerc is a stupid player. He'll buy in at a table for $100, lose the whole stake, slide off the chair, and cry to his wife: "Boy what a rotten run that was." Then he laughs. What a jerk he is. Didn't he realize he was in a bad streak? Did he have to lose the whole $100? He should have read that bad streak sooner.

Same is true when you get into a good trend. You've got to be able to take advantage of it. Lee Tillslow is a little slow in grasping when he is in the middle of a scorching run.

He'll win twenty-three out of twenty-five hands, turn to his wife and say: "Boy, am I scorching, this dealer is ice cold."

She'll ask him how much he won. The big reply: "Oh, I popped 'em for about $125."

A hundred and twenty five dollars?? Can you imagine this sap sitting at that table, getting the run of his life, and glowering over a handful of chips? He should have been closing in on a grand. Good Money Management methods would have allowed him to take full advantage of that run.

You'll get good trends, but you have to know when you're in the middle of one so you can take a full shot. Don't wait until its over to bemoan your stupidity.

Go back over the chapters on the Regression System and the Up and Pull Theory. They show you how to pull back profits while increasing your bets during these hot streaks. The chapters on Plateaus give you the keys for when to increase your series bets.

It's a strong part of Money Management, being able to take advantage of streaks. If you don't, the constant bad trends will destroy you.

Heed my words.

MONEY MANAGEMENT

19

Charting

I want you to look at this chapter and grasp what I'm saying. If you believe that trends dominate in gambling, you'll have an easy time applying charting.

I believe in charting very, very, *very* strongly. So you get an idea of what I think of this part of your day.

It entails checking out the dealers to find one in a losing pattern. Sometimes it'll take hours to find a cold dealer. So what?

Would you rather play against a hot dealer and lose? Or search out a cold dealer and have a chance of picking up a percentage return?

They'll be plenty of people who disagree with this theory and claim that charting is just a waste of time.

On my TV show, there is always a skeptic who'll call in and claim that he doesn't buy this move. He'll say that there are times when he'll chart a table, catch a cold dealer, buy in, and lose four straight hands.

Sure that will happen. Just like you big Romeos who will spot a beautiful lady in a restaurant, check her out for two hours, get the come-on, make your move, settle in for a big score, and get shot down for all your efforts.

Is that going to deter you from future scouting missions? Of course not. Sometimes you win and sometimes you lose.

But if you took a shot at every table or every lady you passed during a given day, I guarantee your losses and shoot downs would multiply. You have to check out situations.

I'm only asking you to grasp the reason you chart: To find a dealer going cold during a certain time period and avoid taking on a dealer who is scorching hot. Charting is a powerful move.

MONEY MANAGEMENT

20

How to Chart

You know why you chart, now let's get into how. Since all your decisions in Blackjack are based on your two cards against the dealer's up card, then that's where your keying begins.

Stand at a table and watch what card the dealer is showing as his initial up card. If he is continually showing a 9-10-Jack-Queen-King-or Ace (power cards), then the people at that table are in plenty of hot water.

Trends run with players, along with dealers. A lot of times I'll sit at a table and hear the dealer say: "Man, I've been ice cold all day." That's music to my ears, because I love dealers who are running bad.

So your charting will call for you to watch that up card of the dealer to determine his patterns.

I want him turning over 2-3-4-5-6 because then you can double and split against him. The 7 and 8 as his up card combination is considered neutral. He is neither weak nor strong. The 9-10-Jack-Queen-King-Ace are considered power cards and he'll probably whack you.

Let's say this dealer shows a 5-Queen-9-3-Ace-10 as his up card over a six-hand run. There were only two times I would have had a shot at him. I'd pass on that table. Go chart another game.

Next table I see 9-Jack-Ace. I don't even wait for a fourth hand. This guy's scorching and again I pass.

Next table shows 4-9-5-7-Jack-3-4. That's where I'll play. In fact if he turned over three straight lousy cards (5-3-6), I'd have jumped right in.

Don't chart for more than ten hands at a table because if he's going to show a pattern, he'll be in one sooner than nine, ten, or eleven hands. He's probably chopping, so walk and find the guy who's showing 60% or 67% or 70% bad, weak up cards.

Yes, you'll chart sometimes, find a cold dealer, lay your buy-in money on the table, start to play, lose four straight hands and begin cursing the day you heard of charting. It'll happen, but my intent is to get you geared to playing only where the dealer is cold.

I am 100% tuned into strong charting techniques, and hope you'll read, grasp, apply, and use the power of charting. It will get you playing at and against dealers who are bobbing and weaving. Then whack 'em!

MONEY MANAGEMENT

21

Money Management Message

This will be quick, short and to the point. It'll also irritate you to the point you may even be disgusted with my theories. So be it.

Gambling is a rough business and not a playground, a place to kill a few hours, and drop a few thousand.

It's a place where you have a shot to win some money if you play like the professionals do.

That means having the *Big 4*: Bankroll, Knowledge of the Game, Money Management, and Discipline. It means being aware of the *Little 3*: Theory, Logic, and Trends.

It means using the Regression Money Management method, Charting the tables, breaking money into Sessions and most of all the setting of Win Goals and Loss Limits.

It also calls for you to apply Plateaus and Guarantee and Excess moves as you progress in your hot streaks.

In other words, all of these things must be a part of your day, or you haven't got a prayer.

If you apply all of them, you have a shot. A 50–50 shot. If you don't or won't get or won't use all of these things, then *stop gambling*.

'Nuff said.

MONEY MANAGEMENT 22

Establishing a Goal

Since Money Management is so important, it stands to reason that it is hard to follow. There are so many restrictions placed on the player that the temptation to deviate is always present. There are plenty of reasons why guys want to chuck Money Management, and all of them enter each player's mind at various times.

I preach Money Management, and this is the primary tool that most gamblers lack. I lay out the rules and expect the players to adhere to them. Most people who gamble have a tremendously difficult time adhering to any type of control.

As I said before, Money Management puts lids on every player, regardless of his bankroll. The temptation is always to take the shot at going for the big kill. The $100 player goes for it, and so does the $3 bettor. Their goals are the same, but obstacles leap out at both types.

The high roller starts with a $5,000 bankroll, and when he wins $3,000, it is never enough. Even $5,000 winnings aren't satisfying. He wants the $10,000 and $15,000 payday. And many times when that comes, he still isn't happy. In fact, this guy has plenty of money to play with, and actually never will be satisfied. He has absolutely no idea how to win.

The $3 bettor has a $300 bankroll and dreams of the $3,000 score. But with such a small bankroll, it is very, very rare indeed that he can even come close to those figures.

In reality, both of these types should be content with a percentage return on their starting bankroll, and quit when they reach it.

When I run seminars, I insist that players set a Win Goal of

20% of their starting figure. Realistically, this is a high return, but try telling nonprofessionals that. They think doubling their money, in one day, is almost considered a losing proposition.

A professional gambler is content to win 10% of his starting cache, but the novice gambler merely scoffs at that figure. For that reason, I make the 20% return the goal, and in all honesty, this is a high figure to expect to extract from the casinos on a regular basis. But the novice cannot condition himself to lower returns, and since there absolutely has to be a set goal, this figure allows us to at least set an amount to shoot for.

I love it when a person comes in and readily admits he will accept a 10% return on his money—as long as we can show him how he can do it consistently. These types are a joy to work with. They are so obsessed with trying to break their losing habits, that any type of winning is a bonus to them.

I have said this before, and it bears repeating. You have absolutely, positively, no right to decide on your Win Goal. Your bankroll makes that decision. Did you digest that last sentence? I'll repeat it. It is the first, and maybe the second most important part of Money Management (after the ability to walk). Your bankroll makes the decision as to your win goal.

As long as I have indicated that I will condone 20% winnings in my seminars, that is the figure I use in this book.

You know how much you are bringing to the casinos, and that figure is your bankroll. If your bankroll is $1,000, your goal for the day is $200. Not a bad day's pay, for doing something you enjoy. If you bring down $600, then your goal is $120. If you bring down $300 then $60 is the goal, and don't go getting hyper, that is too low a return. You want to win more? Bring more! You haven't got more? Then you have a simple choice. (1) Don't go, or (2) go with the $300, and accept $60 profit, and be happy when it comes.

I've actually had people openly decry this 20% goal. They ridicule it, and claim it is not worth the effort. What a ridiculous analogy. These people have simply not learned how to win.

You want to set higher win goals? Go ahead. Personally, I think you're crazy, as a Win Goal is not a win limit, and you do have options, which we will cover.

But, if you want to set higher win percentages, that is your option, or theory. And remember what I said about theory? All good players are entitled to their own theories, and who is to say who is right or wrong? It is my theory that a 20% return is an excellent goal to shoot for.

You make your own figure, but at least make a figure, don't make it a ridiculously high one, and stick to it.

If I were to go out on a limb and give you a higher percent to shoot for, and if you twisted my arm real hard, and held a gun to my head, and promised me Raquel Welch's phone number, I could be persuaded to radically increase my expected win percentage to—21%!

There, I said it, and already I'm sorry. I think it is just too high.

I think you get the point. Twenty percent, period.

MONEY MANAGEMENT 23

Summary

Now do you know about Money Management? Please understand how important it is. I agree it is very restrictive, but therein lies the reason the casinos are able to beat the daily gambler. So many people refuse to properly manage their money while gambling. They are never fully aware of how much they would be content to win, or in the case of losing, they never set a limit on how much they will allow themselves to lose on a given day.

Believe me, it is just as important to restrict your losses, as shown in the session, as it is to set goals on the winning side.

But, setting these limits and goals is one thing. Following them is another. If you insist on gambling, regardless of what game it is, you have to set rules, and follow them. Don't be impatient and don't be greedy.

If you ever do master all of the rules set up during the chapters on Money Management, the changes in your approach to the game of Blackjack will be dramatic.

Give these changes a good, long chance to work. It is said that something worth having is worth working for. Well, try to master the art of consistent winning at Blackjack.

If you follow the system of breaking your bankroll into sessions, and your sessions into series, you will be on the right road to a Money Management method.

You then set you Loss Limits at 40% per session. The win percentage will be 20%, and when that is reached, break it in half, and work with the excess.

As long as you keep winning with the excess, you stay at the table.

When the excess is gone, so is your session.

Set Loss Limits, and keep them. Set Win goals and reach them.

Knowing when to end the session is the strongest mark of the professional gambler.

A player sits at a table with $200, and wants to walk away with a 20% profit.

He plays for about an hour, never getting more than a $25 profit, nor any worse than a $30 deficit. Finally, he gets a good run of cards and now has a profit of $70. Right there is the crucial part of Money Management. Take that $70 and guarantee yourself a profit. Put aside $35 as your "pay" for that session. The other $35 is your excess. The initial part of that session is over. You can never touch your session start-up money of $200, nor the first $35 again. You are positively going to leave that table a winner. The excess $35 will be used to play with. Every time you win a series, half goes aside as additional profit, and half stays with the excess. This keeps you playing at a lucrative table.

The same is true of your series. When you hit the fifth or sixth straight win of a series, don't be ashamed to drop back down to a lower bet.

You can keep that series alive, and now you can become extra aggressive. The key to this whole New York system is learning how to win.

It's a profitable experience.

DISCIPLINE

1

Icing on the Cake

Discipline. This is the part of gambling that destroys almost all bettors. Ninety-five percent of the people who gamble do not have discipline.

If you don't have it, and you refuse to acquire it, you will never win at gambling. I can't make it any clearer.

Remember how I suggested that you set a Win Goal and stick to it? Well, that's very difficult to do. The professional gambler would love to win $15,000 every night. But if he only has a starting bankroll of $1,000, how can he set such lofty figures? The answer is simply that he doesn't set those high goals. He bases his win goal at 20%.

When he reaches that realistic figure, it is very simple for him to put $100 in his pocket, and play with the other $100. That is discipline. Setting rules, and following them to the T.

That doesn't mean he is finished for the night, but it does mean he has guaranteed himself a profit. Naturally, his original bankroll can never be touched again that night. Nor can he dip into the $100 he set aside as his "pay." But, the $100 he kept out, to put into play, that becomes his "stake." There is no limit as to how high he can run up his excess winnings, but he can play, content in the knowledge that he will leave the casino a winner!

By the same token, discipline works on the other side of the coin. You must set loss limits in gambling. My figure at Blackjack is 40%. If I lose 40% in any one session, I'm gone! That's it, the session is finished. What's the use of playing down to that last chip? What's the logic in it?

I hear an answer way out in left field: "Maybe you'll get

lucky, and run that last chip into $3,000—my brother's-uncle's-wife's-cousin once took a $2 chip and turned it in-to!!!"

Ever hear a story like that before? Of course you have. Because it happens. But they are isolated cases. As soon as I hear someone begin to tell me a story of someone he or she knows who won a great deal of money, I get speechless. I know there is nothing I can say that will ever convince the storyteller that discipline is important.

Once a person turns a small bankroll into a fortune, or even hears of someone doing it, he figures it'll happen again. I can never reach him with logic. When I try to tell him that winning 20% is quite a feat, he turns me off, and refuses to listen. It's too bad. People want to win so badly, yet never want to pay the price.

Look at the lottery. In New Jersey, every time somebody cracks it for a big killing, people pour into the stores, buying bundles of tickets, hoping they'll be the next recipient. It's just human nature.

People want that big kill, that million dollar jackpot.

Stop chasing the rainbow! Set limits for yourself, and minimize your losses. Acquire Discipline!

Set an amount to take to a casino. Don't go there with every dime you can scrounge up. Don't go there and blindly keep drawing on your credit line. Go with an amount that you have set aside to gamble with. That's *Discipline*.

Break your bankroll into sessions. That's *Discipline*.

Chart a table like I showed you. Use patience to find the one that suits you, especially where the dealer is running cold. That's *Discipline*.

Bet your session money in series, depending upon the starting figure. That's *Discipline*.

Play Basic Strategy the way it's shown on the charts. That's *Discipline*.

Leave the table if you lose 40% of your session money. That's *Discipline*.

Leave the table, if after you have won a certain amount, and split your winnings, the excess is then lost. (Don't touch your winnings.) That's *Discipline*.

These are a few of the rules to follow. Yes, it will be hard, and yes, it will take you time to master it.

So, start now!

DISCIPLINE

2

Discipline Applied to the Author

While I'm on the subject of Discipline, maybe a little background on the author would be appropriate.

Many years ago, I discovered gambling by the way of poker games in garages, and at parties, and then betting on pot games in bowling. It was very easy to win.

I practiced very, very hard to perfect these "skills," and then branched out into other fields.

A friend brought me to Monmouth Park, and opened a whole new world to me. Why, this was a cinch. I'll come every day, make a fortune, and never work again.

Handicapping the horses became an obsession. I worked hard, and studied hour upon hour. There would be big days, and there would be lousy days.

Eventually, I started going every day, but had now reduced my betting down to only one or two races a day.

The next challenge was the biggest of all, sports betting. I never dreamed you could actually bet on the outcome of a football, or basketball, or baseball game. It was another world to conquer. My entire day was wrapped up in charting the various teams, and deciding on a winner.

By now, I was engulfed in gambling. It appeared so easy. I never made big, gigantic hits, but never got completely wiped out. When I did lose a bundle, it was always offset by winning at a poker game, or in a bowling match.

By now, the die was cast. I was looking for more things to bet on. I read all of the books on Las Vegas, and since I knew the the basic idea behind Craps and Blackjack, I figured I was an expert at those games as well.

Roulette intrigued me. In fact, the whole idea of Las Vegas pumped me up. I figured: "Why not go after the big kill in the gambling capital of the world? What not go to Las Vegas?"

For months I saved, putting together a bankroll of $3,000, and worked on a system in Roulette that would revolutionize gambling. I figured I was such a genius, they'd probably ban me as soon as I started "milking" all the casinos with my system.

The big day came, and off I went, $3,000 in my pocket, a dynamite system in my head, and the knowledge that I was a fantastic gambler. I'd knock them dead, those donkeys out in Vegas. I'd show them what a real gambler was all about.

Sure I would!

On Wednesday, I arrived in Las Vegas. Wednesday night, I started my system. Friday, I was broke. Saturday, I was working as a shill, for $10 a day.

You don't want to hear the gory details of my demise. It'd make grown men cry. It made me cry.

The years passed, and I bounced, and bounced, and bounced, and bounced. One day up, the next day down.

I learned that you need money to compete: A bankroll.

I learned that you'd better be an expert in the game you play: Knowledge of the Game.

I learned that even with a bankroll, you'd better know how to control it: Money Management.

I learned that there are trends in betting, and that when you win, you'd better walk: Discipline.

Isn't it funny? Sounds like the *BIG 4*. Well, it took me years to realize it. Many years of hard work, and disgust, and happy times, and rotten days. Having hot rolls on the dice, and then fighting red hot dealers in Blackjack. Realization came slowly. How come there were so many days that I was ahead so much money, and still left the casino a loser? I had no Discipline. None. I didn't know how to win.

My dad always said: "There's nothing thicker than a thick Irishman." No doubt about it, I sure was thick.

When reality finally hit, it took many years to perfect the Discipline. Seems all of the other factors were fairly easy to acquire, but Discipline took some doing.

I remember one day in particular, when I was pushing very hard to make Discipline work for me.

I was armed with a small bankroll, about $1,000, and had set my win goal as $200 per day.

Well, this one particular morning I walked into the California Club in downtown Las Vegas, and in fifteen minutes had won $200.

It was about 9:15, and I had already made my goal for the day. The rules called for me to stop.

I left the casino, proud as a peacock, and decided to relax for the day. I had breakfast, and went to an 11:00 movie. I think it was *West Side Story*.

When it was over, I came out, had lunch, and decided to kill a few more hours at another movie.

I came out and it was about 4:30. Now what do I do? If you've never been in Las Vegas, this will sound like a crazy question. Try walking around that town, and not being able to gamble.

But I was determined to follow the rules of stopping when I hit my goal. It was a rough job, not being able to go to a table. But I made it through that night and that could have been a beginning.

I continued setting Win Goals and Loss Limits. My approach to gambling took a complete 180° turn. Sure, it's exciting to bet a great deal of money on the turn of a card. But the losing, which can happen, eventually gets to you. It was a rough, tough transition.

I eventually acquired Discipline. It is still very hard to follow the rules. It is still so tempting to take a whack at a ball game, or a Craps table when the urgency of making a killing engulfs you.

But, you know the comforting factor? I enjoy the winning. I enjoy the consistent wins, even if they are small. I am not "destroyed" after a losing day, because my bankroll can never be depleted. Not when I limit the losses to a percentage of my bankroll.

Hard? Is it hard to have Discipline? You can bet your sweet life it is!

But it sure helps you win more often.

And that beats losing.

Anytime!

DISCIPLINE 3

What Is Discipline?

There's nothing mysterious about the art of Discipline. Everyone needs it, in every walk of life.

Can't you just picture a schoolteacher, armed with eight years of grammar school, four years of high school, four years of college, two years for a master's degree, and two more for a doctorate in mathematics, teaching fifth grade students about basic arithmetic?

The tremendous amount of knowledge she has must be repressed, so she can reach the level of her students. The temptation is to fill their heads with her wealth of knowledge. But Discipline must be used. She has to bring them along slowly, not belt them with things that will overwhelm them. That's Discipline.

A guy painting a house, on a contract basis, has the homeowner's guarantee of payment on a written document. He knows he's going to be paid when the job is finished. But he can't paint that house in two days. He must scrape and smooth every nook and cranny on that house, preparing for a neat paint job. The temptation to rush the job, grab the money and run, is always there. But do a couple of rotten pieces of work, and you'll not be hired again. So, he has to learn to practice Discipline, taking his time, and making sure his work is good enough to get return engagements. That is a form of Discipline.

You must discipline yourself to accomplish almost anything you do. Why not, then, in gambling? Why not, in a game you know so little about? Why is it that people just cannot admit that they know nothing about the proper way to win at gambling?

I give lectures to various clubs, groups, and organizations on the subject of gambling, usually casino games. The people I meet are simply awed by the fact that they know so little about the games they play, and particularly Money Management and Discipline.

They offer various excuses for why they cannot exhibit Discipline, all of them ridiculous. The most common excuse for not practicing Discipline, is the statement: "Well, I only go down to the casinos twice a year, and I don't want to be governed by any rules. I figure I'll contribute my $300, and have a good time while I'm there."

In the next breath, they'll ask: "But how come I always lose? Isn't it possible to win sometimes?"

These people want to win, but go to the tables with ideas that prevent any chance of winning. They play to lose, thinking they can't win. Even when they get ahead, they feel it's an accident, and give it back.

Discipline is the hardest thing to accomplish in a casino. It is completely restrictive. Most people who gamble dream of big killings, and multi-thousand dollar paydays. Discipline doesn't prohibit big wins, but, calls for a lot of caution, and, as a result, is primarily designed to provide small wins.

Discipline is an art rarely practiced by people who gamble. The ones who are way ahead, throw caution to the wind, figure they are playing "with the casino's money," and shovel their bets in wildly.

The people who are losing, forget to restrict their losses, figuring they are "due" to win. They double up, hoping for a change in their fortunes. If you are cold on a certain day, you'd better realize that you could stay that way for a while.

The best thing to do when you're losing consistently, is pack it in. Cash your chips and wait for another day.

That's self-control. That's Discipline.

DISCIPLINE 4

The Plunger

You think this guy has Discipline? Well, if you've never seen a person with no Discipline, look for the plunger. They're in every casino, at every racetrack, involved with all types of gambling.

They're called all types of names—plungers, high rollers, money men, black chip bettors, anything that sets them aside from the $5 bettor.

When they win, it is always for thousands of dollars, and when they lose, they go for a king's ransom. They plunge their winnings back into the game, always going for the big kill.

The casinos love these high rollers. That's why they are showered with rooms, meals, tickets to shows, and first class treatment. The people who run the casino are no dummies. They realize that feeding the ego of these high rollers, with a few complimentary gifts, keeps these players coming to the casino.

The casinos know that the more these players are favored, the more they will bet, never being content to win just a percentage of their bankroll.

It is a never-ending circle, with the bankroll of the house matched against the lack of Discipline of the big roller.

I hear people talk in awe of these players they see betting huge amounts at the table. It is the everlasting dream of every bettor to one day "break the bank."

At the other end of the spectrum is the big bettor himself. In private, these people tell me that they have lost interest in betting $25 and $100 chips and are now bored, unless they can bet $300 and $500 per hand. These are men with families, bills, jobs, and not professional gamblers.

One particular guy, we'll call him Mal, is a regular visitor to Atlantic City. In the beginning, he went to the $10 table, but soon found that unless he was betting at least $25 a hand, he was bored.

Soon, it took the $100 and $200 bet, at either Blackjack or Craps, to hold his interest. Recently, he told me of his latest escapades in Atlantic City.

He is now into Baccarat, and was up $5,600, with a $1,000 buy-in. He was betting $500 per hand, and he said he had dreams of winning $100,000. The bottom line was that he lost the $5,600, plus the $1,000 buy-in.

The kicker was his comment to me, that he is now bored with Blackjack, and wants only to play Baccarat for $500 a hand. He loves the attention that betting big gives him. He has become a plunger, and has absolutely no Discipline at all.

He is not a compulsive gambler, does not bet sports or horses. He is a very good Poker player and Blackjack player. But, and this is the worst part, he has no Discipline, and has lost sight of any type of control in the casino. He privately admits to me that he doesn't know how to get up and walk. Do you think he will ever be a consistent winner? Definitely not.

I know it. The casinos know it. And he knows it. That's a plunger! And he has no Discipline.

DISCIPLINE 5

The Professional Gambler

It used to be a dirty word: Professional Gambler. Everyone pictured a rough looking cat, a scar on the side of his cheek, hat pulled down over the yes, and dressed in black, from head to toe.

The idea probably began back in the days of Humphrey Bogart. But it is very far from the truth. I won't say there are a tremendous amount of professional gamblers, but there are people who make their livings gambling.

Most of them take up residence in Las Vegas, where gambling is legal, and they are able to place bets at any time of the day or night.

The thing to remember about professional gamblers is that they do not get that classification by default. They have to earn it. It is a glamorous life when you are winning, but it is a lousy existence when you are losing. That is why the word professional is placed in front of gambler. The gambler, who makes a living by betting on sporting events or horses or casino games, has put many years into learning his trade.

You can be sure he has Discipline. He'll walk away from a game as soon as things start to go against him. It is absolutely imperative that you do not go broke on any given day. You must have money to be able to compete the next day.

When casinos in Atlantic City first opened, people who had never bet in a casino before raced down, won a couple thousand dollars, and proclaimed themselves professional gamblers.

Try doing it over a period of ten years, and then come and tell me about it.

Almost every week, somebody will ask me how to become a

professional gambler. To be honest, not everyone has the makeup to take the beatings that must come in this way of life.

For instance, the professional gambler, who concentrates on the races, must be at the track every day. He must know about every single, solitary horse on the program.

He will not just go to the track once or twice a week, and the rest of the time take his information out of the newspapers. No, he is at that track, sometimes at 5:00 A.M., watching the various trainers putting their horses through their workouts.

When the actual handicapping begins, it will take approximately one hour to chart each race. Naturally, the pro will not bet on every race. He will eliminate those contests that give him the least chance of winning. For instance, let us say the professional horseplayer wants to eliminate about four to five races on the card. The following stipulations are applied, and if there are such races scheduled that day, he merely crosses them off:

Twelve-horse fields
Maiden races
Claiming races of less than $10,000
Races for two-year-olds
Any race with more than seven horses
Any grass race

These are just a few of the rules that the pro *may* set for himself. On the three or four races left, he will get into his serious handicapping. If he doesn't see something that he believes will give him a good chance of winning, he will pass. Sometimes two or three days can go by without a bet being made.

That's Discipline, but it is also following your own strict set of rules, and attempting to make your wagers only when you feel you have an excellent chance of winning.

The novice will rush into a track, bet four or five horses in each race, trying to find reasons to bet every horse, and sometimes be broke by the fifth or sixth race.

An odd thing about professional gamblers, many of them will not bet on every facet of gambling. Many of them concentrate on just one or two categories. They do not spread themselves all over the board. Some concentrate on only one, maybe Poker, maybe Sports, maybe Craps.

Then again, there are those who have five or six different areas in which they like to concentrate. But you can be sure they are experts in every category.

You may wonder why I mention a professional gambler in a section on Discipline. I am trying to show you the comparison between the pro and the weekly player. Blackjack is a very, very tough game to play. You think it is merely to get as close to 21 as you can, then pray that the dealer breaks?

Thousands of people rush to a casino and take their best shot with a bankroll that could be put to better use. They get $400 or $500 to the good, and it is still not enough. They want more, and more, and more. No end. And when they do stand to lose, they feel their luck will change back and all control is thrown out the window.

The professional gambler will go into the same casino and have incredibly strict limits on how much he will lose on that particular day.

He will also have that all important goal, and when he reaches it, he is absolutely, positively, guaranteed to leave that casino with a profit.

I want you to examine your own gambling methods. Do you know the game as well as the professional? If you don't, then you'd better learn it, if you want to play. If you are a great player, why not put the same strict Discipline factor in your repertoire of talents. If the pro can do it, so can you.

I'm not trying to make you a professional gambler. I'm trying to get you to copy some of the traits that they have. If even one tiny bit of advice rubs off on you, it will help perfect your game.

The one thing you should have to be a professional gambler is a strong stomach. It seems every single ball game, every card game, every horse race, appears to go down to the final tick of the clock. Do you know how many ball games I have lost on the last shot? Hundreds, and each one is like a Joe Louis smash to the gut. It hurts, and it hurts bad. But you have to put it out of your mind and attack the next game. But those losses do take their toll. Can you put up with that? Think about it! The professional gambler has to.

DISCIPLINE 6

Learning How to Win

You've heard me use the term over and over: "Learning How to Win." This is not an idle statement. It takes a strong, disciplined person to both learn how, and then continue to know when he has won.

You've probably been turned off by the low percentage returns that I insist you adhere to. If every single person who walked into a casino set a 10% return factor on his bankroll, you would see some serious head-shaking by the casino bosses.

Do you realize that approximately 70% of the people who gamble in a casino are ahead at one time or another during the course of a day? Furthermore, of the 70% of the people who do get ahead, 90% of them kick the money back in. In other words, they get ahead, but instead of walking away, they play on and on, looking for bigger kills.

Getting ahead is not hard. But the amounts of money that people want to win is just out and out preposterous. The stark reality of losing money does not hit you until you leave the casino and head for home. It finally dawns on you that you were ahead a couple of hundred dollars and gave it all back. Worse than that, you gave back the money you came with, and just to put a little icing on the cake, you used your line of credit at the casino for an additional $500, and that also went down the drain. Your day ended with a tidy little deficit of $1,000. Add to that the amount you could have won, maybe $300, and you have a swing of about $1,300. And now you also have to worry about paying off that marker.

You think this doesn't happen? If you had your house mortgage with you, that probably would have been thrown into the fray.

Everything loses its perspective when gambling comes into play. Money becomes chips. People who put 25 cents in the Sunday church collection, make $5 bets for dealers who are complete strangers. A guy who won't buy his wife a new refrigerator, gets ahead $200 and bets $100 a hand on the next two deals.

Who are you kidding? Where's the control with these people? Nowhere!! They have no control, no Discipline.

I sit at Blackjack tables and see guys get a couple of hundred dollars ahead, and pour it right back to the casinos.

Learning how to win means exactly that. As soon as you get ahead an amount of money, based on your starting session amount, there is no way in the world that you should leave that table a loser.

Almost everyone knows of Pete Rose, the former baseball great for the Cincinnati Reds and Philadelphia Phillies. Before his gambling troubles, he was renowned for having great hustle and desire, and for the fact that he overtook Ty Cobb for the most hits in a career.

Pete Rose did not go out and bang thirty home runs a year. He learned to become what is called a disciplined hitter. Sure it's a great thrill to hit one out of the park and have the fans scream in delight. But, Rose learned early in his career that he did not have the physical capabilities to consistently hit home runs. He adjusted and became a contact hitter. He played within the confines of his ability, and he was successful. Most fans admired Pete Rose as a baseball player (as a gambler is another matter—he is the perfect example of a gambler who lacked Discipline).

I've been telling you over and over to do the same thing in gambling. Play within the confines of your bankroll.

I know you'd like to step up to a Blackjack table and knock the stuffings out of the game and hit a home run. Well, if you don't have the bankroll, you can't do it consistently.

Play with what you have, and win within the limits of your starting stake.

When you get ahead, put some money aside, so that when

you slide off that chair, you take some of the casino's money with you. Once you get into the habit of winning, it will become contagious.

Learning to win is an art—a time consuming, difficult undertaking. It is hard because we are all engulfed in a constant straining to be successful. Winning to some people is not satisfying unless it is such a high amount that it will gain the admiration and envy of our peers. But the plain fact of the matter is that most people who gamble do not come to the games equipped to win consistently. They should be thankful to get ahead, and smart enough to run with the profit.

Learn how to win! I don't care how much it is. The amounts can increase as your starting bankroll increases. For now, learn how to get ahead, and get out of the casino with the profit. After awhile it will be second nature.

DISCIPLINE

7

A Hard Core Percentage

I want you to decide on what will be the exact percentage of your bankroll you will accept as a winning session.

Before you walk into a casino is the time that decision must be made. Well, start thinking about it right now.

I tell you that 20% is the proper amount. If you are thinking in terms higher than 30%, you will find this a pretty tough mountain to climb.

As I have explained to you in the chapters on Knowledge, Blackjack gives you about an even chance of winning each hand, based on religiously following the Basic Strategy chart. In essence, you are playing an even game, and getting ahead is tough enough without setting goals that are too difficult to achieve.

Take six months out of your helter skelter brand of gambling. Set intelligent hard core goals that are easy to achieve. Set the 20% win goal and stick to it.

Set the 40% loss limit on both your bankroll and your sessions. This will cut down greatly on your losses.

You will have losing days. Everyone does. It's part of the game. But minimize these losses. Keep them small so you are back in action the next day.

Until you learn to set these percentage wins and losses, you will be a constant loser.

Spend a half hour a day on the chart until you master it. Go over the Money Management methods until you are perfect. You will become a player. You will become a winner.

And finally on the bankroll. Don't visit a casino until you

can play at the various levels I have set up. The bankroll will give you the time—and the hard core percentages will govern your wins and losses.

DISCIPLINE 8

A Couple of Stories

I have been gambling for twenty-five years. Sometimes I win; sometimes I lose. But, I enjoy it as much today as when I first got my feet wet. The losses still hurt and the wins are always satisfying. Like I have said, the learning took a long time, but discipline has finally engulfed me. My losses are never staggering, and I will always be ready to go the next day.

I'm afraid that is not the case with people I meet every day. In my seminars, I try to get to know every person. My phone number is always available to them to call for help, or to discuss their play.

When I hear from these people, it is usually with plaudits as to their finally acquiring Discipline, and the ability to walk away.

Several years ago, only a few days before Christmas, I received a call at about 3:00 in the afternoon from Mike S. He was in Atlantic City and he phoned just to tell me he was up about $400, and was heading home. Mike won $400 the previous Friday, and he walked. On the day he called, he won another $400. He had his money and was walking away from the tables. He called for only one reason. He wanted to tell me how easy it was getting for him to be able to win and get up and leave.

I have known Mike for almost two years. He came to me as a complete novice, straight out of college. In the beginning, it was a thrill for him to win $50. Then greed overtook and almost destroyed him. He saw how easy it was to win, and he started shooting for higher and higher payoffs.

Oh, he won. But then *it* happened. The trend reversed itself, and Mike got whacked. We talked almost daily. He has regrouped and relearned how to win.

Four hundred dollars is not going to excite all you big hitters, but the amount is irrelevant. The bottom line is winning.

On that particular day that Mike called, he mentioned Discipline. He said he realized he didn't have Discipline, only after he got ahead and pushed the money back to the casinos. The times he won, he took for granted. The losing sessions made him realize how many times he was up, and refused to leave. Mike is an excellent player who is now putting the finishing touches on his game. If he stays at it, the casinos will have a rough time getting into his bankroll.

Several years ago, while I was in Las Vegas, I was in one of my losing streaks, and just killing time walking downtown.

I went into the Fremont Hotel and heard a buzzing around one of the crap tables. I walked over and saw right away what the attraction was. Some guy was betting $2,000 a shot on the Don't Pass line. I couldn't believe my eyes. It was one of my close friends, a guy named Arthur. Arthur was as broke as I was. In fact, a few nights earlier, he an I took a bus ride into Los Angeles so we could get a few hours sleep for $2. That was the cost of a round-trip. We didn't have money for a room, so it was a nice place to grab a few winks.

It turns out that Arthur put a few bucks together and got into this craps game. He caught a cold table and started shoveling it in.

Anyhow, the game progressed and Arthur continued to add to his winnings. Finally, a slight, gray-haired gentleman picked up the dice and placed a $1 chip on the Pass Line. My buddy Arthur pushed $4,000 on the Don't Pass line. The man threw a 10. That means to win his dollar he needed to make another 10 before a 7 showed. Arthur needed a 7 to come before a 10 to win $4,000. Arthur then laid $8,000 odds against the 10. That means he was betting a total of $12,000 to win $8,000. He was betting that a 7 appeared before a 10.

If you know Craps, you know that there are only three ways

to make a 10 (6–4, 4–6, and 5–5), as opposed to six ways of making a 7 (6–1, 1–6, 5–2, 2–5, 4–3, and 3–4). That means Arthur had a 6-to-3 (same as 2-to-1) chance of winning his bet. The odds were in his favor. Luck wasn't.

The shooter came right back with a 6–4. He made his 10, and won a dollar. Arthur lost $12,000. The hush at the table was deafening.

Arthur shrugged his shoulders and walked away. I followed him. A few minutes later, he stopped at another craps table and started digging into his pockets. He came up with a $1 chip and placed it on the Don't Pass line. He was starting all over at the bottom of the mountain.

I walked away, but that incident remains very vivid in my memory. What was Arthur looking for? He had his Utopia when he reached $12,000, but still he couldn't stop.

Where is Arthur today? I don't know, but I'll bet he's still searching. Maybe he learned Discipline. His actions that day helped me. It was one of the hundreds of things that I have seen during the years that give me insight into the things that people will do in a casino.

DISCIPLINE 9

Attitude

By now you know that there are two types of people in a casino: The Expert and the Dope. You can decide which line you'd get in.

A lot of the rotten habits that people have in a casino revert back to how they perceive gambling. A guy heads for the tables with an attitude: "Who cares if I win or lose, I'm really only down here to have a good time."

That is a stupid analogy of what gambling is all about. Yet people have that outlook. It's a lack of Discipline.

Discipline is hard to acquire, harder to put into play, and still harder to retain. The animal instinct in all of us cries out to "go for the kill." And rarely will you get scorching hot runs that will give you gigantic returns.

I'm asking you to change your attitude about gambling. Approach it as a job, as a means to make money. You must want to win, and you have to believe it's possible to win. Mostly you must quit when you do reach an intelligent profit, based on your starting Bankroll.

Twenty percent is an intelligent amount, although a bit high. Soon you'll realize what a great feeling it is to win and you'll get to approach the tables with confidence.

Play to win—don't play to play.

Finally, let me again refer you back to the chapters on charting, Win Goals, and Loss Limits.

You'll get into the habit of winning and accepting small but consistent returns. And your attitude on gambling will change. Especially the part where you think it's only an exercise in contributing money to the house. It's not.

DISCIPLINE 10

Losing Days

Earlier in the book in chapters on Win Goals and Loss Limits, I stated that they were two of the most important messages you could apply to gambling.

Right now in the Discipline section, I'd like to zero in on one of these situations: "What happens on losing days?"

Get it into your head right now that you aren't gong to win every day. You can't. It's a virtual impossibility. You've a better chance of having the Playmate of the Month call you three times a day than of winning every day you gamble.

And she isn't going to call you three times a day.

So when you're locked into a losing day, you must have the guts to abide by those Loss Limits and wrap it up for that period. Even it it means turning tail and heading for home after only two or three losing sessions.

Losing days will occur and there is nothing you can do about it. That's because trends dominate and a losing trend can last for hours, so don't fight them.

The disciplined player will realize he's in a losing trend, pull in his horns, and minimize those losses.

Remember: It's not how much you win at gambling—it's how little you lose.

You have to hold the losses down to preserve your bankroll for the days you're in a hot trend. That's when you make hay.

Fighting losing streaks by staying at that table or betting higher, is like a fish swimming upstream. Neither one of you is going anywhere.

Losing days will happen. So be it. Just be sure you realize it quickly, pull back and walk.

That's Discipline.

DISCIPLINE

11

Reality

A lot of you won't like this chapter because you won't want to agree with the message. It's an honest look at your chances of winning at gambling.

To have a 50–50 chance at Blackjack, you must have a strong bankroll, which calls for a session amount to be thirty times that of the table minimum. You must be perfect at Basic Strategy.

You *must* have a powerful Money Management method and impeccable Discipline. I'll bet the family jewels that most of you fall by the wayside on a couple of these necessities. Maybe all of them.

Yet if you don't have all of these things, you don't have a prayer of a chance of winning consistently.

And if you do have all of these things, you have no better than a 50–50 shot. That's the reality of gambling. Yet thousands of people flock to the world of gambling with dreams of making big kills.

Dream on, my friend; you're in fantasy land. But you have a lot of company. Approximately 75% of the people in the casinos think that gambling will give them the supercolossal windfalls that will change their lives. Baloney!

Those dreams are unrealistic and if you think they aren't, think back over your past trips to the tables. How many times have you walked away with profits up in the high four figures?

So why not give my conservative style of play a good strong look? All I want you to do is look for percentage returns at a game that's only offering you a 50–50 shot. That Win Goal percentage is 20% and should be easy to reach. It's also a bit more realistic than looking to double and triple your starting stake. And that's the cold, stark reality of it.

Gambling is rough and the dorks who think they'll start with a few bucks and win thousands, have lost touch with reality.

DISCIPLINE

12

Wrapping It Up

If you have come this far in the book and still don't understand what Discipline is, then it's going to be a long time before you become a consistent winner. I have shown you the percentages to stick to, and the danger signs for alerting you that it is getting close to walk time. If you follow these few basic steps, you are gong to experience some new thrills in Blackjack:

1. Set your Loss Limits and Win Goals outside the casino.
2. Loss Limit should be 40% per session, and 40% of your starting bankroll. Not a penny more. But, you can quit anywhere up to 40% if you see you are fighting a hot dealer.
3. Win goal should be 20% of your session, then split the 20% profit in half and play with the 50% excess. The other 50% is set aside to guarantee a win for that session.
4. Divide you bankroll into three separate sessions of equal value.
5. Break your sessions into series bets, always making the first bet of a series higher than the table minimum, and then, after a win, regressing the second bet to the table minimum.
6. Leave a table if you lose the first four hands.
7. Chart a table before you sit down.
8. Never sit at a table unless you have at least thirty times the amount of the minimum.
9. Realize what a rough game Blackjack is and play only

when you have perfected the *BIG 4*.
10. Learn how to win. Learn to walk when you get ahead.
11. If you lose, learn to walk when your losses reach 40% of your starting bankroll. No excuses.
12. Learn *DISCIPLINE*!!

If you can force yourself to adhere to these few basic rules, you will be on the way to becoming a strong player.

Finally, discipline is tough to acquire, and hard to maintain. But since it guarantees results, it is worth the effort.

If you don't think Discipline is rough to perfect, just listen to what Webster's Dictionary says about it:

". . . Chastisement by way of correction and training; hence training through *suffering*."

Yes, you will suffer a little, but the fruits of victory taste very sweet. I hope you get a great big mouthful.

ODDS AND ENDS

Synopsis of the Big 4

Well, you've come full cycle on the *BIG 4*. I hope you're still with me, and a little wiser, to boot. Like I've said, it's tough to decide which one is the most important, as they all rely on each other to maintain a steady course towards winning. But, if really pressed for an answer, I would lean toward one of them as the absolute necessary ingredient toward the winning formula. Before I divulge my choice, let me finalize each of the categories:

Bankroll Don't think you can play Blackjack with a short amount of money. If you go with a short bankroll, you will play scared and your whole betting scheme will suffer. Bankroll is the catalyst. It is your starting block and throughout your sessions, you will play comfortably knowing you have the money to sustain yourself during down trends. You must have the proper bankroll. For the beginning, I suggest $600, but would accept $450. Remember, the most you can lose is 40% of that amount, but start with the numbers I suggest.

Knowledge of the Game As I've said, everyone thinks he knows the proper moves to make in Blackjack, but look over the figures of that survey I mentioned. Every Blackjack player should follow Basic Strategy, and that includes the moves that scare you. I know it's rough to hit a 16 versus the dealer's 7, but in the long run it is going to produce more wins than losses. If you don't know Basic Strategy and it is broken down in detail in this book, then you shouldn't go near a Blackjack table.

Money Management Just for fun, go into a casino and pick out any single Blackjack table in the house. Stand behind it, and watch the various betting methods of the players. See if you can spot patterns to their betting procedures. Probably you won't notice any consistent system at all. Every person should have at least a method to increase or decrease bets after winning or losing a hand. If you play without a system, you are only treading water. There must be set patterns to follow, otherwise you will never take advantage of hot streaks, or be able to control cold streaks.

I believe the regression/progression (212) system allows a tremendous amount of leverage to your Blackjack playing. It gives you control of your money at all times and provides plenty of options for both the conservative and aggressive player. Money Management is a necessary factor if you expect to win at gambling. If you won't practice it, you will never become a consistent winner.

Discipline   This, in my humble opinion, is the most important item of the *BIG 4*. Eventually, you will pick up on the other three, but acquiring Discipline and then using it is quite tricky. Your own mind will keep giving you reasons to stay at a table long after your winning trend has disappeared. People find it very difficult to win money in the casino. Yet, realistically, it is almost an even game they are combating, so the blame should be placed right where it belongs—on the shoulders of the player. If you are a bad player, you are not going to win. If you get ahead and continue to try and break the bank, you will continue to lose. When you get ahead in a casino, there is absolutely no reason why you shouldn't leave a winner. That is why I warn you that until the glorious art of Discipline engulfs you, you will lack the most important ingredient of all. If you think you will never acquire it, then quit gambling today.

THE BIG 4   I've touched all the bases. Now it is your choice as to how badly you want to win. Or, do you just want to continue to play for the fun and excitement that gambling allows?

I sincerely hope you have gained something from these pages, and that you will apply some of that knowledge to your future Blackjack play. Remember the main thing that I have stressed over and over. *Learn How to Win*! Get into the habit of tearing yourself away from the table when you are ahead.

The amount that you win is not important. It is based upon your starting bankroll. As the bankroll increases, your session wins will likewise increase.

SO YOU WANNA BE A GAMBLER?

Get the necessary *Bankroll*!

Absorb all of the *Knowledge of the Game*!

Learn *Money Management*!

Acquire *Discipline*!

The path leads to *Winning*!

ODDS AND ENDS 2

Tipping

A touchy subject. So how do you approach a touchy subject? Go right at it. No holds barred. No beating around the bush! Get right to the point, and let the chips fall where they may.

You tip for a purpose. You tip to thank someone for a service, or a job performed. Well, the dealers in a casino do not make a lot of money. They depend on tips to determine if they will have a good income that week.

They want you to tip. Some of them are very courteous by nature, and it is very easy to tip them. Some are out-and-out boors, and treat you as an intruder at their table. I have seen people tip rude, surly dealers, hoping to get them in a good mood.

Forget it. If you have a dealer who is obnoxious, don't tip him. What did he do to earn your tip?

Do dealers favor players who tip them? Of course they do. Let's assume seven people are playing at a Blackjack table. One guy is tipping and the other six are not. Whom do you think the dealer is pulling for? Not only because he wins when you win, but because he wants to keep that guy at the table.

How do you tip? Simple. Just place a chip about five or six inches in front of your bet. You are signalling the dealer that he is now playing your hand for the amount you place on the layout for him.

How much do you tip? At a $3 or $5 table, a dollar chip is acceptable. If you are winning, a bet for the dealer every six or seven hands is OK. If you are losing, why tip, unless you are trying to grease the pan?

Let me approach that in layman's terms. You are hoping that

the dealer will make a mistake in your favor. The pit boss (who was once a dealer himself) looks away and the dealer beats your 17 hand with his 18, but calls the hand a push, no bet. No loss and no bet. Another time, you have 19 and he has 19, but he miscounts and pays you by mistake. It happens, but rarely.

Don't underestimate the intelligence of the people who run casinos. They know all the tricks of the trade. They can walk up to a Blackjack table, watch five hands, and evaluate every player in the game. It is their job, and they are good.

Do they cheat? Of course not. They don't have to. The casinos give you a fair chance to beat them. But, they are well aware that everyone does not come equipped to take them on.

Some people lack the bankroll, some lack the knowledge of the Game, some have no Money Management, and most have no Discipline. And without all of those *BIG 4* items, you haven't got a chance.

No, the casinos don't cheat, so put that thought out of your heads.

A final word on tipping. It's not a bad idea. If the dealer does not show appreciation, you can move or stop tipping.

By asking for white (dollar) chips, you are signalling the dealer that you are a tipper. When you get ahead a few dollars, test the waters. He will also help you in making decisions.

I have seen people play for several hours and they start to get bleary-eyed. Some will stand on an Ace, 5. Others call for a hit on a hard 18. I have seen some people miscount a soft 21 (Ace, 4, 6) and call for a hit.

I have seen some dealers give the player a hit. A sharp dealer will remind the player that he has 21.

Become aware of these things in a casino. You want to tip? Go ahead. You will get the dealer's attention. What happens from there on is called cat and mouse. (Make sure he doesn't turn out to be a rat.)

ODDS AND ENDS 3

Streaks—Hot and Cold

I strongly believe trends dominate gambling: Hot and cold streaks, hot and cold hands, hot and cold dice. Patterns that can suddenly shift and head a successful session towards failure—and vice versa.

They are impossible to explain, but these trends keep popping up.

You have probably noticed when gambling that you constantly run into streaks. When streaks run in your favor, you brag how smart you are. When they go against you, it's "lousy luck." Well, instead of blaming them, learn how to take advantage of these streaks.

You will find these streaks, or trends, occur often in gambling. Learning how to handle them will work wonders for you.

A hot Blackjack dealer appears to do no wrong. How can there be only 5's in the deck when he hits 16? The fact is that he is "on a roll." Don't fight it. The easiest and smartest thing to do is to walk away. Leave the table. Don't argue that he is "due" to get cold and you will beat him eventually. Nonsense! There is no reason to sit and ride out his hot period when your enemy has everything in his favor. Leave the table and start a new session somewhere else.

Look for the cold dealer. When you do, you'll find yourself constantly winning four, five, and six in a row. That's when you start pouring in your bets. If he's cold—go for the casino's jugular vein. You'd better, because you must make your hot streaks pay off to offset the bad times.

Since all dealers have hot and cold runs, check around until you find a dealer who is struggling.

I do it by charting the dealer's hands. I merely go to a table, but don't sit down. I watch the dealer play five to ten hands and use his up card to take his temperature. Hot or cold?

When the dealer shows a 9, 10, Jack, Queen, King, or Ace—you are in trouble. The 7 and 8 are neutral, but I consider them weak. The 2 through 6 indicates he is in trouble.

For the next ten hands, the dealer's up cards are 7, Queen, King, 5, Ace, 9, Jack, 4, Queen, 9. That means the players sitting at this table must deal with seven strong cards: Ace, King, two Queens, Jack, and two 9's.

Why sit at this table? Why buck a dealer who is turning over a larger amount of strong cards than weak ones? It's tough enough to beat the house when the dealer is winning the average number of hands, fifty-one to forty-nine. Don't fight the extra burden of a hot dealer.

Skeptics will argue that if you do sit down at the table, the dealer's up card will change. That's true. I am not saying he will turn over the same card. It's obvious that a new player changes the hand.

What I am saying is that your presence at the table won't necessarily cool off the hot dealer. Since he is already hot, walk to another table and begin charting all over. Wait until you find a pattern of more weak cards than power cards.

A ratio I look for is six weak cards in ten hands, or four straight weak cards, or three weak cards in five hands. If there is such a pattern of more weak cards than power cards, sit at that table.

What have you got to lose? Certainly not your money if you find the right table.

ODDS AND ENDS 4

Does Luck Count?

If I had a dime for every time someone asked me this question, I wouldn't have to gamble again.

Luck has no determining factor in gambling, and surely not in Blackjack, where it is hard enough to win, even if you're perfect in Basic Strategy.

So many people honestly believe that luck will carry them through. Let's face it, everybody has luck. Some people have good luck, some have bad luck. But to risk your money at Blackjack with the excuse that you are a lucky person is simply ridiculous.

When I work Bingo at night at the church where my daughters go to school, I see many women put their "lucky charms" on the table. I ask them why they do it. Their answer is that it brings them luck. A couple of times, after noticing that a lady didn't win, I would jokingly go over and suggest that she change her lucky charm. Sometimes my wit was not taken in the vein in which I intended.

One time I saw a woman suffer through an unusually rough night. I was clearing the boards off the table as she was packing up. All of a sudden, she took her "lucky charm," which was a small metal elephant, and screamed: "You won't bring me any more bad luck." With that, she turned and threw the elephant as hard as she could. It went right through a window in the hall, shattering glass all over the place. Her temper would cost her a couple of dollars for the window.

I told her that her lucky piece was still working for her. "You broke one of the small windows and it could have been the big pane glass. So your luck is running good."

Funny, she never spoke to me again. But carrying good luck charms is just a matter of superstition. It will never help you win a bet.

Personally, I don't believe luck has anything at all to do with winning or losing. A good poker player, or gin rummy player will beat a poor, lucky player over and over. The same is true in Blackjack. You can get hot and win several hundred dollars a couple of times. But, in the long haul, skill and knowledge is needed.

Don't trust luck to carry you through. Acquire knowledge, and study the best percentage moves. Above all, remember one basic rule: Don't depend on small metal elephants to carry you through.

ODDS AND ENDS

5

Bad Player at Third Base

Forget the myth that has been handed down through generations of Blackjack players. It concerns the player sitting in the last seat, or third base as it is called. So many people seem to think that his decision as to whether to hit or stand is going to affect the whole table. Well, it does, but so does every other player's moves at the table.

The problem is that you always remember what the last player did for two reasons:

1. Your attention span is so short, you can't think back two hands.
2. If you lose, you need someone to blame, so why not the poor guy in the hot seat?

This question comes up over and over. It's uncanny how many people want to believe this nonsense. I agree that it would be nice to have a strong player at third base, but it would also be nice to have a strong player in every seat. In the crammed casinos in Atlantic City, where there are so many novices, you are likely to find five or six out of seven players at a table. You have two choices. Either don't pay attention to them, or leave the table.

In your everyday lifestyle, don't you tend to look for someone to blame for something that happens?

- In baseball, the guy who makes the last out, even though he had four previous hits.
- In bowling, the fellow who misses in the tenth frame, even though he ends up with a 233 game.
- In football, the quarterback who finishes the game with

three straight incompletions. Forget the fact that he threw four touchdown passes and scored two other TD's. We have to blame someone.

- In bingo, I've seen groups of women organizing lynch mobs to hang the guy who calls the numbers. Forget the fact that he has no control over what number the air blower shoots up. The thing is, he isn't calling their numbers so they have to blame someone. Why not this poor guy?

- In the department store, how many times have you sworn at a salesgirl because you thought an article was priced too high? You knew she had no control over the amount, but you have to level your wrath on someone.

- Even getting a little ridiculous, haven't you ever heard a little ten-year-old girl claim that the teacher doesn't know what he is talking about, especially after the little tot receives a failing grade in spelling? She has to blame someone!

I am trying to make a point that we should approach gambling the same as we approach anything we do in life. Take it seriously, or don't go near it. It's just a part of our makeup to look for excuses. We don't like to blame ourselves, so we look for the scapegoat.

In blackjack, it's the guy at third base. But, you know, in the long run, the decisions he makes will hurt you sometimes, and help you on other occasions. It's just that you tend to remember the ones that go against you.

Personally, I like to sit at first base, as it is very, very easy to count from that position. Sometimes I notice what the person at third base is doing, but usually I am interested just in counting. How the other players at the table act is none of my business.

I am well aware that the majority of players in a casino are poor gamblers. But, I don't have the right to dwell on their inadequacies. If they bothered me, I wouldn't play at their table. But, the bottom line is that it really doesn't faze me.

You should feel the same way. If a player makes moves that irritate you, either don't watch him, or leave the table.

Incidentally, while I'm on the subject of bad players, examine the person throwing the rocks. How is *your* game? Are you perfect? I don't mean good, or very good, I mean perfect!!!

If you aren't, put down the rocks.

ODDS AND ENDS 6

Fast Dealer

You see them in every casino. It seems like they are going for a world's record in speed dealing. Admittedly, dealing Blackjack for eight or ten hours a day becomes very boring. But, if you are at a table where some hotshot dealer tries to impress you with his speed in dealing out of that shoe, you should either leave the table or purposely slow him down.

As I have said many times during the course of this book, over 90% of the people who frequent gambling casinos do not know what they are doing.

It takes many of them several seconds jut to count the total shown on their first two cards. To arrive at a decision in a split second when confronted by a fast dealer will reduce this person's play to a guessing game. And guessing, or hoping, or assuming, has no place in gambling.

In my seminars, I want everyone to be able to give Basic Strategy answers in a fraction of a second. I'll place one card face up on the layout. Maybe it will be a 4. That represents the dealer's up card. Then I'll take two decks of cards and turn them over face up, two at a time. These two cards represent the player's hand. The player must be able to go through two decks in one minute, giving the proper move for each hand against the dealer's 4. Perfection is required. Why not? Why not be perfect at the game?

These speed drills make you automatically aware of the proper percentage move to make the instant you see your two cards against the dealer's up card. I agree that you have a few seconds when you are seated at the table, but being pretty good at Blackjack is not good enough, and if you do not become perfect at Basic Strategy, you may alter your decisions some-times, based on a hunch. The speed drills force you to instan-taneously make the proper percentage move, and, win or lose, you are making the move, that in the long run, gives you the least chance of losing.

There are thousands of people who are subjected to fast dealers without benefit of speed drills. After an hour or so, they cannot make correct snap decisions.

I always go out of my way to slow down these sharpies. When I get my turn to make a decision as to whether to hit, stand, split, or double, I take about thirty seconds to act like I am trying to decide what to do.

The dealer knows what's happening and it infuriates him. But he also knows that dealing fast frustrates many patrons. He figures it is his shortcut to a job as pit boss. It isn't.

If a dealer is too fast for you, slow him down. Or, better still, leave that table. If you were charting the table as I showed you, you would notice the fast dealers and avoid them. At any rate, don't let a dealer buffalo you with fast dealing. He is not on your side.

ODDS AND ENDS 7

Reality Again on Blackjack

We're winding down this book now and have touched on all the things you need to have, just to stay alive at the tables.

By now you should realize that I take gambling seriously and don't cater to that idea that visiting a casino for fun or enjoyment or pastime or entertainment or any other stupid illogical reason, is an intelligent move. I say it's a job.

Either you gamble to make money or stay out of my world. Whether you can accept this advice is your own preference, but I'm trying to save you money.

If you're serious about Blackjack, then realize what a tough game it is and why you need to be so proficient.

And don't hand me the garbage that you don't have the time or patience to perfect a game you only attack once or twice a month. If you're risking money, regardless of how few times you do it, you're gambling. And if you're not perfect at that game, you're gonna lose—more times than you win.

That's something I'm trying to get you to do—avoid losing.

The reality of it all comes down to you understanding how tough it is to win and that you're out of your league if you don't play like the pros.

Think about it.

ODDS AND ENDS 8

So You Wanna Be a Gambler?

Alright, the way to play is all laid out for you, but most important is the way to bet and the suggestion to walk with a profit. Only you can force yourself to follow these Money Management and Discipline techniques.

But if you wanna be a gambler, and Lord knows it's a rough undertaking, I hope you realize that to come into this world, you better have all of the things that this book calls for.

My advice would be to swing over to Craps or Roulette or Baccarat as they offer better opportunities of getting streaks at the table. But whatever game you zero in on, be sure you know everything about it, and don't think you're an expert just because you can spell it.

Follow my Money Management and Discipline rules and watch how your trips to the casinos reduce losses and get you in on hot streaks.

So You Wanna Be a Gambler??? Well, be the best you can be.

Everything I've said in this book is directed toward the Ultimate Goal—winning. That's what gambling is all about.

I've shown you how to win. It's up to you to put together a bankroll and play toward that goal.

I've covered the basic approach to Blackjack. As of this writing, I have other books and twenty videotapes covering all the casino games, delving into the all-important aspects of Money Management and Discipline.

You pick the game and concentrate on both the basic and advanced concepts that I preach.

It ain't gonna guarantee a winning day every trip to the

casinos because that's an impossibility, but I give you a strong disciplined theory that will reduce losses and point you toward the Ultimate Goal—winning at gambling.

The Ultimate Goal should always be winning, not entertainment at the tables. It's a job. Treat it that way.

Let me leave you with this thought: It is possible for you to become a consistent winner. Please, please don't play until you learn the game, and then play within the confines of your starting bankroll.

You will learn how to win—and you will love it. Since I don't believe luck works in gambling, I'll merely wish you . . .

Happy Winnings,

John Patrick

Claridge Casino Hotel
invites *you* to a
Friendly Overnight Get-A-Way!

You and a guest can enjoy our hospitality for a midweek overnight stay, Sunday through Thursday. Now through December 27, 1992 we have a special rate of $35.00 per person, double occupancy. To make your reservation, call Lorraine at 1-800-442-GAME. And to get the action going ...a *$10 coin bonus* for you and your guest!

Rules: Non-transferable. Offer based on per person, per night double occupancy. Limit one reservation per invitation. Must be at least 21 years of age. May not be used with any other offers. You must make advance reservations. Reservations are subject to availability. Tax and gratuities are not included. Offer valid for midweek (Sunday through Thursday arrivals) now through December 27, 1992. Fridays, Saturdays and holidays not included.

Claridge
Atlantic City
Because smaller is friendlier.

$10   *FREE COIN BONUS*   **$10**

Redeem this coupon at the Casino Promotions Booth on the mezzanine level. You must present a completed CompCard GOLD application and Claridge Casino Hotel room key.

Offer valid now through December 27, 1992. Non-negotiable. Non-transferable.
Not valid if detached from book.

#2795

Claridge
Atlantic City
Because smaller is friendlier.

$10   *FREE COIN BONUS*   **$10**

Redeem this coupon at the Casino Promotions Booth on the mezzanine level. You must present a completed CompCard GOLD application and Claridge Casino Hotel room key.

Offer valid now through December 27, 1992. Non-negotiable. Non-transferable.
Not valid if detached from book.

#2795

Claridge
Atlantic City
Because smaller is friendlier.

Present this coupon with a valid same day parking stub and a valid bridge/toll receipt at the casino promotions booth on the mezzanine level between 10:00 am and 2:00 am daily to receive a coupon good for $10.00 in dollar slot tokens. No more than (4) people per parking stub and bridge/toll receipt. Will accept line bus tickets in place of parking stub and bridge/toll receipt from any casino other than the Claridge. Offer not valid with any other offers, discounts or bonuses. Management may change or cancel this offer without notice at their discretion. Claridge is not responsible for lost or stolen vouchers. Casino employees are excluded from this offer. Alterations or unauthorized use voids this offer and may lead to criminal prosecution. You must be at least 21 years of age. No cash value. No partial redemption will be given. One coupon valid per person. Not valid if detached from book.

Guest Signature

Present this coupon with a valid same day parking stub and a valid bridge/toll receipt at the casino promotions booth on the mezzanine level between 10:00 am and 2:00 am daily to receive a coupon good for $10.00 in dollar slot tokens. No more than (4) people per parking stub and bridge/toll receipt. Will accept line bus tickets in place of parking stub and bridge/toll receipt from any casino other than the Claridge. Offer not valid with any other offers, discounts or bonuses. Management may change or cancel this offer without notice at their discretion. Claridge is not responsible for lost or stolen vouchers. Casino employees are excluded from this offer. Alterations or unauthorized use voids this offer and may lead to criminal prosecution. You must be at least 21 years of age. No cash value. No partial redemption will be given. One coupon valid per person. Not valid if detached from book.

Guest Signature